INTUITIVE EATING

+

Emotional Eating

A Revolutionary 4-Step Program, Based on 10 Principles, That Works! How Thousands of People, Rewiring Their Minds, Stuck to Their Diet and Have Lost More Than 125 Pounds

By **Meredith Carney**

INTUITIVE EATING

A REVOLUTIONARY 4-STEP PROGRAM, BASED ON 10 PRINCIPLES, THAT WORKS! HOW THOUSANDS OF PEOPLE, REWIRING THEIR MINDS, STUCK TO THEIR DIET AND HAVE LOST MORE THAN 125 POUNDS (PART 1)

By **Meredith Carn**

TABLE OF CONTENTS

INTUITIVE EATING

A REVOLUTIONARY 4-STEP PROGRAM, BASED ON 10 PRINCIPLES, THAT WORKS! HOW THOUSANDS OF PEOPLE, REWIRING THEIR MINDS, STUCK TO THEIR DIET AND HAVE LOST MORE THAN 125 POUNDS (PART 2)

By **Meredith Carney**

TABLE OF CONTENTS

EMOTIONAL EATING

Break the Cycle, Say STOP Binge Eating! A Proven 21-Day Program Based on Ten Intuitive Principles for a Healthy Relationship with Food. Be Free from the Slavery of Hunger (Part 1)

By

Kelly Francis

TABLE OF CONTENTS

EMOTIONAL

EATING

Break the Cycle, Say STOP Binge Eating! A Proven 21-Day Program Based on Ten Intuitive Principles for a Healthy Relationship with Food. Be Free from the Slavery of Hunger (Part 2)

By

Kelly Francis

TABLE OF CONTENTS

author or publisher.

Disclaimer Notice:

Please note the information contained within this document is for educational and entertainment purposes only. All effort has been executed to present accurate, up to date, and reliable, complete information. No warranties of any kind are declared or implied. Readers acknowledge that the author is not engaging in the rendering of legal, financial, medical or professional advice. The content within this book has been derived from various sources. Please consult a licensed professional before attempting any techniques outlined in this book. By reading this document, the reader agrees that under no circumstances is the author responsible for any losses, direct or indirect, which are incurred as a result of the use of information contained within this document, including, but not limited to, — errors, omissions, or inaccuracies.

Foreword

This integrative function illuminates how reasoning, once regarded as a "purely logical" setting of thinking, is in fact, reliant on the non-rational processing of our anatomies.

Knowing a little about the mind can help to realize why we're born with the wisdom we have to become Intuitive Eaters. Additionally, it may help us to observe how we're in a position to live an Intuitive Consuming life, even while becoming bombarded by the endless options of organic and refined foods open to us every day and the relentless diet plan messages that abound.

Human beings are privileged to see a dynamic interplay of instinct, emotion, and the mind mediates idea, which interacts to orchestrate life, and so. Mindfulness and psychiatrist expert, Daniel Siegel, M.D., calls this technique "Mind-Sight." There are three parts of the brain accountable for this powerful integration.

The first region is named the reptilian brain, since when the first reptiles roamed the planet earth; they acted and responded by instinct exclusively. They didn't rationalize, or feel-they merely went for this. As life evolved, another degree of brain function developed, called the limbic mind, which mammals possess also. Emotions and interpersonal behaviours originate right here. In the human limbic brain, feelings are layered upon the instincts of the reptilian mind. The abilities from the reptilian mind are delivered to the human limbic brain, which serves to increase consciousness. Ultimately, the third key area of the mind evolved, known as the rational mind, or the neo-cortex. The sensible human brain integrates instincts and emotions from the additional two brain regions. The sensible brain will not control instincts-instead; it perceives the instinctual and feeling elements of our beings and displays upon them. The rational mind creates thoughts and vocabulary.

Intuitive Eating embraces most three elements of the human being brain. In toddlerhood and infancy, eating is instinctual mostly. As we get older, thoughts and feelings frequently play a part in our decisions about eating. As we frequently tell our clients, our bodies are not only composed of the tongue and the stomach but the mind also. We've often heard somebody say, "I believed that as an Intuitive Eater, I possibly could eat whatever I needed. So, now I consume whatever I'd like and in so far as I want, whenever I think like it!" In fact, this comment distorts the premise of intuitive feeding. Yes, make peace with meals, and consume what pleases your palate. Yes, provide yourself with the freedom to consume unconditionally, and eat just as much as you need to fulfil the body. But eating once you experience it, without respect for food cravings and fullness may not be an extremely satisfying experience and can even cause physical pain. Attunement, together with your body's satiety cues is usually an important part of the process.

As an Intuitive Eater, you'll be honouring your brain, because it is a component of the body. As you feel the concepts of Intuitive Eating, you'll be storing info in the memory "files" that you produce and house in the human brain. When you are feeling hungry, you will have to pull up a number of these files, while deciding what things to consume. You will evaluate how starving you are feeling and then consider what foods might fulfil your hunger as well as your taste buds. You may actually go through a number of sensual imaginings of the flavour and texture and heat of different foods. You may open the file to reflect on past eating experiences also. You may inquire yourself whether your current eating choice spent some time working out for you personally when you've consumed it previously. Achieved it sustains you very long enough? Achieved it makes your bloodstream sugars crash? Did you finish up with indigestion? Or do you thoroughly benefit from the food and want it again? Your feelings may also come into play when you have the desire to eat. Might you become upset and so are craving foods to comfort and ease and soothe yourself? Or are you bored and considering feeding on as a distraction? Considering these options might inform your decision about what things to eat, or even whether to consume/eat at all.

Initially of your trip to reclaim your Intuitive Eater, you will likely be hyperconscious of hunger, fullness, satisfaction, thoughts, and emotions. The human brain should be extremely in tune together with your tongue as well as your stomach. As you become even more adept at recognizing your internal signals, you might find that your instincts and intuitive wisdom consider even more of a prominent part in your eating encounter. Therefore, Intuitive Eating is actually about trusting you will be capable of accessing all the information you must have, by using all the areas of your brain-your reptilian instincts, your limbic reference to your emotions, as well as your rational thoughts.

Through Intuitive Eating, we figure out how to trust the wisdom which has always been within but has been blunted by years of self-doubt. Doubting their innate consuming signals had prolonged to doubting their beliefs about a great many other areas of their lives.

We've heard stories about individuals who have left abusive associations, made peace with estranged family members, and also have made significant profession changes, once they have a problem with meals and body has been resolved. We have also found out about new romances that, for a few, could not have already been possible while these were occupied with body issues and focused on the most recent doomed diet plan attempt. Intuitive Eating offers freed most of these people to continue with their lives while departing behind self-question and despair.

Introduction

I f you could profit every diet just like a frequent flyer program, the majority of us could have earned a vacation to the moon and back. The almost $60 billion at 12 months, the weight-loss industry could finance the trip for generations to arrive (Bacon and Aphramor 2011). Ironically, we appear to have significantly more respect for our vehicles than for ourselves. If you took your vehicle to a car mechanic for regular tune-ups, and after money and time spent, the automobile didn't function, and you wouldn't blame yourself. Yet, regardless of the fact that 90 to 95 per cent of most diets fail-you have a tendency to blame yourself, not the dietary plan! Isn't it ironic that with an enormous failure price for dieting-we don't blame the procedure of dieting?

Initially, whenever we ventured into the globe of private practice, we didn't know each other. Yet, separately, each folk had remarkably similar guidance experiences that triggered us to rethink how exactly we work. This resulted in a significant change in how exactly we practice and years, later on, was the impetus because of this book.

My objective for Intuitive eating wasn't fame or fortune, however. When I sat right down to write the book, I simply wished to educate and motivate visitors to achieve superior health, whether they wished to lose weight, feel good, or invert a chronic disease. I experienced no idea the publication would take off, or that it could resonate so deeply with people all over the world. It seemed everyone began using that phrase-intuitive eating-to explain the overwhelmingly effective eating design detailed in reserve. And to this full-day, there are apparently never-ending blasts of discussions, describing miraculous health adjustments, caused by this topic.

The trick behind Intuitive eating's popularity is easy: It didn't promise an instant fix. Unlike crash diets that guarantee easy and instant results, "Intuitive eating" organized vital details about food and healthful eating that allowed visitors to be specialists in nutrition. The publication essentially paid to its visitors the keys to effective weight reduction so that these were in charge of their health destiny.

Center to Intuitive eating is a straightforward health equation, the core idea of my nutritarian program:

H = N / C Wellness = Nutrients / Calories

Your wellbeing is predicted by your nutrient intake divided by your calorie consumption.

I contact this core idea the nutrient density of your daily diet. Food gives us nutrition and calorie consumption (energy). All calories result from only three components: carbohydrates, fat, and proteins. Nutrients, however, come from noncaloric food factors, namely, vitamin supplements, nutrients, fibres, and phytochemicals, actually chemical substances that generally occur in plants. These noncaloric nutrients are quite crucial to your wellbeing. When the ratio of nutrition to calorie consumption is high, fat burns up, and wellness is restored. The even more nutrient-dense meals you consume, the, even more, you'll be happy with fewer calories, and the much less you'll crave excess fat and high-calorie foods.

A high-nutrient diet decreases growing older, helps restoration cells, reduces inflammation, and helps rid your body of toxins. High-nutrient, low-calorie foods include a great deal of dietary fibre and take up a whole lot of space in the stomach. As you consume a more substantial quantity of food, it satiates your food cravings and blunts your hunger.

Meeting the body's micronutrient requirements also helps suppress food craving and what I contact "toxic hunger, " which drives you to consume more calories than you require -usually in the type of processed foods, which can result in cancer and heart disease, among a great many other ailments.

Witnessing how Intuitive consuming inspired a lot of people to improve their diets not merely reinforced my results that high-nutrient diets create good wellness; it offered a considerable, ongoing body of proof proving that approach works. Nothing displays the energy of this method of consuming more than hearing from individuals who apply this understanding and live it each day in their personal lives. Thousands of individuals lost dramatic levels of weight without problems rather than regained it. One reader called Scott weighed an astounding 500 pounds. Scott couldn't tie his very own sneakers. His breathing was laboured, and he could walk only nine actions at a time. He was thirty-eight years aged. A doctor informed him that if he didn't undergo belly reduction surgery, he'd probably die within half a year. Scott spurned his doctor's guidance and instead made a decision to switch how he considered food and his method of eating by pursuing my high-nutrient meal strategy, which offered him with the nutrients, protein, and vitamin supplements he had a need to achieve good wellness. Because he right now eats for health, he can eat just as much as he wants, ignoring the scale fully. Today, Scott weighs 180 pounds and wants to exercise-a big differ from when he could not walk.

My individuals routinely lose up to 20 pounds through the first six weeks of changing their diet plan. And that's simply the start. More importantly, they typically get over diseases such as for example allergies, asthma, acne, headaches, high blood circulation pressure, diabetes, reflux esophagitis, lupus, kidney insufficiency, psoriasis, angina, cardiomyopathy, and multiple sclerosis-and they steadily get to get rid of their dependence on prescription drugs.

Though I have very long studied and utilized high- nutrient eating as a medical prescription for days gone by twenty-five years, actually I must admit to being amazed by a few of the phenomenal recoveries folks have reported if you ask me. Once, somebody asked whether this micronutrient-rich approach could change their hair back again to brownish from grey. "Of program not really," I answered. But, affirmed, on my website discussion board, two different people commented that it experienced occurred to them. I couldn't believe it. Similarly, among my sufferers had hepatitis C prior to starting my eating design. I didn't believe this high-nutrient eating design would remedy his hepatitis contamination and liver injury; nevertheless, after some right time, his hepatitis C disappeared. I had to do it again the blood tests 3 x to believe it. Seeing such dramatic recoveries from what exactly is conventionally considered irreversible illnesses excited me, making me even more adamant that delicious method of eating can result in medical transformations for an incredible number of Americans.

The total results and success stories are astounding. They come from folks of different back again- grounds, from different age groups, and they all began their journeys for different factors. Yet what they talk about in common is all of them are now in excellent wellness. For most of the Intuitive eating's achievement; however, I quickly found realize that science-based details about nutrition only wasn't enough. With these details available to such a wide audience, why would a lot of people neglect to recognize there have to protect their valuable health insurance and lose weight? Why would they become unable and unready to change? Why would they like to reject unassailable, scientific, and significantly effective advice? I'll let you know why, due to the mind-boggling twin powers of meals preference and meals addiction.

Just like the classic victim, we actually grow to love things that kill us-in this case, unhealthy food. Unhealthy eating styles and meals addictions have both used control of our brains, and this dependence on certain foods is frequently as deadly as many other addictions.

The standard American diet plan (SAD) is eliminating us. Rather than providing us with these basic needs once and for all health, it has created a country where disease and persistent illness are believed to be unavoidable and just another organic consequence of ageing. Carrying excess fat is the primary reason behind type 2 diabetes; it accelerates atherosclerosis and death from cardiovascular disease. In just a matter of years, excess body weight is usually projected to overtake smoking as the root cause of loss of life in the USA. By enough time, most Americans reach age fifty, they are already addicted to prescription drugs, and almost fifty per cent of People in America still die of heart attacks and strokes. You don't need to be one of them. Twenty-eight million Americans have problems with the crippling discomfort of osteoarthritis. You do not have to be one of these. Thirty-five million Americans have problems with persistent headaches. You don't need to be one of them. You simply don't need to be sick.

Today, 475 million adults all over the world suffer from obesity. That's a 50 per cent increase since 1980. Simultaneously, the amount of over- excess weight adults is fast approaching 1 billion, plus some 200 million school-age kids are already overweight, which means almost 1. 7 billion individuals are either overweight or obese. One nearly 7 billion people!

In the USA alone, about two-thirds of People in America are overweight, based on the National Institutes of Wellness (NIH). But this doesn't tell the complete story. Both NIH and the Globe Health Business define an "obese" person to possess a body mass index (BMI) of 25. This implies that a woman who is 5 feet 5 inches tall is considered a standard pounds at 150 pounds, and a guy whose 5 feet 10 inches tall is considered regular at 175 pounds. This man and female may carry between 20 and 30 pounds of disease- leading to excess fat around their waists. However, they would be considered healthy and match by today's standards. This is not accurate to look at a person with that very much fat normal or healthy. If you look at societies or groups of individuals who live longer than average, you'll discover average group BMIs between 18 and 22-nowhere close to the American regular of 25. For instance, the Okinawa Centenarian Study-which examined a lot more than 1000 centenarians from Okinawa, Japan, over twenty-five years from the mid-1970s to 2001-found that the common BMI of the studied adults was 20.4; The Adventist Health Study-who follow a mainly vegan diet-found an identical result. This twelve-year prospective study of thirty-four thousand middle-aged and elderly Adventists without preexisting illnesses, no background of smoking, cardiovascular system disease, malignancy, or stroke exposed a primary positive relation between a lesser BMI and longevity. An Adventist with a BMI greater than 23 does experience a higher threat of premature death.

Just what exactly can we study from these studies? Based on the data, the utmost acceptable weight generates a BMI of around 22.5, not 25. This implies that the recommended healthful weight for a 5-foot-10-inches adult male is usually between 130 and 160 pounds, and for 5-foot-5-inches adult female is 108 to 135 pounds. That is a large difference from the suitable (not obese) American BMI of 25, which allows 150 pounds for a female and 175 pounds for a guy. Based on the Okinawan and Adventist regular BMI, about 85 per cent of Americans are overweight, not really the 66 per cent based on the NIH. The common American is definitely heavier and sicker than she or he even realizes. All due to the typical American diet. Hardly anyone can get away its destructive effects. Why else would 90 per cent of everybody older than sixty-five be taking medicines to lessen his or her blood circulation pressure and/or cholesterol? The end result is this: In the event that you eat American meals, you will inevitably develop the illnesses common in America, you shall become overweight, and you will ultimately develop high blood circulation pressure and raised cholesterol (the signs of bloodstream vessel and cardiovascular disease), just like everyone else.

We now contemplate it normal to reduce youthful vigour inside our thirties, carry a supplementary 30 to 40 pounds, live with chronic illness inside our past due forties and fifties, and endure our final years completely reliant on others. But this is simply not normal. This is actually the consequence of a lifelong design of harmful living and misguided info. Instead of dreading deterioration and an increasing number of ailments and medications as we approach later years, we should anticipate enjoying an active existence well into our nineties. This might seem like an outrageous expectation because the majority of us spend eternity eating an unhealthy diet. Today even, too many folks continue to skip the connection between what we consume and how we experience emotionally and actually. Nor can we find out why it appears so difficult to remain at our youthful adult weight.

But it's not as well late.

A high-nutrient diet will certainly reduce your desire to have high-calorie, low-nutrient foods. Within weeks, your taste buds will change, and you'll weary in the processed foods you once believed you could by no means live without. You'll experience more satisfied consuming fewer calorie consumption than you were consuming before. The result is lasting health and long term weight loss. So a lot of my visitors have dropped 100 pounds or even more following my suggestions; they have dropped that much within twelve months, and they have held that weight off for a long time.

THE FINISH of Dieting goes a step beyond Intuitive eating. Not merely does it solution why eating health- completely often appears so difficult, it empowers you with the desire and capability to do so. In the next pages, I talk about the technology and the solutions behind how exactly to rid yourself once and for all of the meals addictions sabotaging your wellbeing. I construct an easy-to-follow eating system you start with a fourteen-day group of easy-to-make, delicious meals that will steadily transform your food preferences, while concurrently recalibrating your palate. I guide your meal options through the first section of the program, so you don't need to think or be concerned in what you're eating-you can merely eat tasty dishes manufactured from fantastic health- assisting foods. In the next area of the programme, I flood the body with nutrition to heal and detoxify it, using very foods in an effort to promote wellness and longevity. By completing and sticking with the program, your BMI shall fall below 22.5 and stay there for the others you will ever have.

A diet can just be looked at successful if the meals you eat helps longevity and protect you against cardiovascular disease, stroke, dementia, and malignancy. This nutritarian diet design is the just dietary and nutritional system that guarantees dramatic excess weight reduction without calorie counting. Additionally, it is the just dietary and nutritional plan that explains how to drive back disease while simultaneously significantly increasing your lifespan. Your threat of a coronary attack and/or stroke will almost disappear, and your threat of tumour can plummet by a lot more than 90 per cent, while your daily life expectancy can boost by two decades. Incredible statements, yes, but that is a reality with substantial scientific support. I've observed such outcomes for a lot more than twenty-five years. Forget calorie consumption. The trick of living well is about micronutrients. Eating healthfully and consuming the proper assortment and quantity of nutrients outcomes in consistent, long-term health benefits. Getting healthful and maintaining well balanced, healthful weights are achieved just by concentrating on the dietary quality of your meal. Contrary to standard thinking, it isn't just how much you take in that determines your body weight; it's everything you eat.

Nutritional quality determines your mental, physical, and psychological health-from brain function and an elevated disease fighting capability to happiness and physical well-being. The primary criterion you should think about when choosing what things to eat is which foods are most favourable to your long-term survival. A diet plan style incorporating longevity- advertising foods enables you to try out all sorts of delicious quality recipes, which allows you to continue this new method of eating through the entire rest you will ever have. Any diet you adopt temporarily only results in short-term benefits because eventually your body and your weight change back to the diet you will remain in the long term. I want to repeat that again: Whatever you adopt temporarily just begets temporary outcomes, and fluctuating your body weight up and down isn't life- span favourable. People often view diet programs as a belief program, picking the one which is most closely aligned with their dietary philosophy or food preferences. They often criticize any system that conflicts with these choices. Real science, however, does not have any philosophy or predetermined agenda; it simply flows inexorably from the preponderance of the data. Are you a scientific thinker? Do you want to view reality and allow chips to fall with the data? Remember: Food choices are learned and may be changed.

We have cared for a lot more than 10 thousand people, the majority of whom set foot in my own office unhappy, sick, and overweight. That they had tried each and every dietary craze without achievement. After following my plan, they found out the superior health they always wanted and dropped the weight they always dreamed of losing. Even better, it was kept by them off. For the very first time in their lives, that they had a feeding on the style that didn't keep them starving or unsatisfied. Most of all, they were in a position to stop acquiring their medicines, which had become unneeded.

In the last three decades, I've reviewed a lot more than twenty thousand scientific tests on human nutrition. For this reason, I can state with certainty that is usually the place and today is the period to begin your wellbeing revival. I've seen the results of this plan doing his thing on a large number of people with a wide variety of diseases and health issues, from migraines and allergies to cardiovascular disease and diabetes. The end result is, it functions. Nutritional excellence may be the most effective way to discover long term healthy weight reduction, prevent and invert disease, and end a few of today's most chronic degenerative illnesses.

Your body is a self-therapeutic machine when you supply it with an optimal nutritional environment, and the information presented in this book is the quickest and most effective way to create that environment. In case you have high blood circulation pressure, high cholesterol, diabetes, cardiovascular disease, indigestion, headaches, asthma, exhaustion, body aches, or discomfort- or if you would like to avoid yourself from developing these chronic conditions- this may be the arrange for you. This fresh diet style can allow you in order to avoid angioplasty, bypass medical procedures, and other invasive methods. In the event that you aren't however ill, it could make sure you do not have heart episodes, strokes, or dementia in your old age. It can reduce and eventually get rid of your need for prescription drugs. In short, it can allow you to optimize your health and potentially save your life. And it could do all this while raising the enjoyment you get from meals.

A lot of you have this publication because you would like to lose weight. I wish to assure you that you'll lose all of the weight that you would like, even if diet programs have failed you previously. This is usually the most reliable weight-loss plan ever, and the email address details are permanent, not temporary. Equally essential may be the protection from severe diseases in your own future that this plan gives. The most efficient healthcare is self-care. Medicines and doctors can't grant you superb health insurance and protect you from disease and suffering. Almost every doctor does know this. The dietary excellence I explain in the following can prevent and actually reverse most medical complications within three to half a year. That is a bold state, but the facts-supported by scientific research-display that lots of the tragedies we encounter in today's world are the consequence of nutritional folly. While weight reduction is important, it isn't our main objective. It is an enjoyable and regular by-product on the path to the principal goal: great health. First-class health is definitely marked by an exceedingly long and fairly disease-free lifespan, and countless research reveals that individuals with superior wellness are thin. By teaching you how exactly to achieve superior health, your ideal weight will normally follow. You will understand the physical cravings that trigger overeating, along with the psychological factors that will help you switch this pattern of usage. Applying the info in this reserve to your life can help you create new, healthy behaviours that may eventually become effortless. You will finally maintain control of your health destiny.

This plan will not include counting calories, measuring food portion sizes, or weighing. It doesn't depend on gimmicks or fads. You can end searching for that magic answer since there is no magic remedy. No reddish berry ketones. No green coffees. No purple tulip nectar or dark salt from the white cliffs of Dover. Actually, we almost always, later on, discover that the merchandise that gave us wish was simply hype and that searching for a magic pill causes harm. Whenever a supplement or medicine doesn't meet up with your nutritive requirements, it really is typically toxic and may enhance the damage the effect of a toxic diet.

As we struggled with these issues, we started to explore a few of the popular literature that suggested a 180-level departure from dieting. It proposed a means of consuming that allowed for just about any and all meals choices, regardless of nutrition. Our preliminary reactions were extremely sceptical, if not down- correct rejecting. We reacted with self-righteous indignation. How could we, as nutritionists (authorized dietitians), trained to consider the connections between nourishment and health, sanction a means of eating that appeared to reject the foundation of our understanding and philosophy?

The struggle continued. Healthy eating plans did not help people maintain long-term weight control; the "nutritional waste strategy" was a dangerous choice. The suggestion to ignore nutrition and disregard the way the body seems in response to eating "whatever you want" discount rates the respect for one's body that comes combined with the gift of life. Finally, we resolved the conflict by developing the process of intuitive consumption. This book may be a bridge between its growing movement against diet and the medical community. While the anti-diet movement avoids dieting and blames body acceptance (thankfully), it often doesn't address health risks. How can you reconcile the problems of forbidden foods but still eat healthy, without dieting? We will let you know how in this post.

In case you are like most of our customers, you are tired of dieting but at the same time terrified of eating. Most of our customers feel uncomfortable within their bodies, but don't understand how to change. Intuitive eating provides a new way of eating that is ultimately hassling free and healthy for the brain and body. It really is an activity that frees the chains of the diet (which can only cause deprivation, rebellion and weight gain in extension). This means getting back again to your roots-trusting the body and its signals.

Intuitive eating cannot only change the relationship with food; it can change your daily life.

Intuitive Feeding on includes the principles of mindful eating; in addition, it has a broader philosophy, addressing the problems of cognitive distortions and psychological eating. It includes seeing realization as a central point in consumption, physical activity/movement in relation to feeling good, rejecting the mentality of the diet, using nutritional information without judging and respecting the body, regardless of how you feel about your shape. Intuitive nutrition is undoubtedly a dynamic procedure that integrates the tuning of the brain, body and meals. For those with feeding problems, conscious and intuitive feeding can help facilitate normal feeding.

CHAPTER 1:

Hitting the Diet Bottom

I just can't get on with another diet plan; you are my last resort." Sandra has been on a diet her entire existence and has understood that she could no longer support a single diet program. She had been with all of them, Atkins, Dukan, The Area, South Beach, grapefruit diet ... too many diets for the details. Sandra was a professional on a diet. Initially, the diet was fun, even stimulating. "Usually, I thought this diet will be different right now." So the routine would be reloaded with every fresh diet, every summer. But the lost weight would eventually be recovered as an undesirable tax bill.

Sandra had hit bottom in the diet plan. At this point, however, I was even more obsessed with meals and her body than ever. She felt silly. "I would have managed and controlled this in the past." What he did not understand was that the dietary procedure had been carried out. Dieting made her even more worried about meals. Diet had made enemy meals. The acquired diet made his experience guilty when he did not consume dietary foods (although she was not officially on a diet). Dieting experienced slowed her metabolism.

Sandra took years to understand that the diet does not work (yes, she knew the emerging idea that the diet does not work, but usually thought it would be different). Some experts and consumers recognize the premise that fast diets don't work: it is difficult for a country of people who are enthusiastic about their bodies to think that even a "practical diet" is often useless. Sandra has been hooked by the interpersonal mythology of the modern age group, the "great hope of diet", for most of her lifestyle since her first diet program at the age of fourteen. At thirty, Sandra felt trapped: she still wanted to lose weight and was uncomfortable in her body. While Sandra couldn't bear the very thought of another diet plan, she didn't understand that the majority of her food problems were actually due to her dieting. Sandra was also discouraged and angry-"I understand everything about diets." Certainly, she could recite calorie consumption and fat grams, just like a walking dietary data source. This is the big warning of losing excess weight and avoiding it usually isn't a problem of understanding. If all we had to have a normal weight was to understand food and nutrition, most people in the United States would not be overweight. The information is easily available. (Take any women's magazine, and you will find abundant diet plans and comparisons with meals).

In addition, the more you try to follow the diet, the more you will fall (it certainly hurts to never succeed in case you have done the best). The best description due to this effect is distributed by John Foreyt, Ph.D., one of the leading professionals of diet psychology. He compared it to a Chinese puzzle (the hollow straw cylindrical puzzle, in which an index finger is placed on each end). The more you try to get out, the more pressure you will exert, the harder it will be to escape the puzzle. Instead, you find yourself locked up in a narrower place ... caught ... frustrated.

Symptoms of Diet Plan Backlash

Diet backlash may be the cumulative side-effect of dieting-it could be short-term or chronic, depending on how long one has been dieting. It can only be one or more side effects. When Sandra got to any office, she already had the traditional symptoms of a violent reaction to the diet. Not only was she tired of following a diet, but she ate less food, but she also had problems losing weight during her new diet attempts. Additional symptoms include:

a. The simple contemplation of starting a diet causes desires and cravings for "sinful" and "fatty" foods, such as ice cream, chocolate, biscuits, etc.

b. When you quit a diet, go overeating and feel guilty. One research indicated that post- dieting binges happen in 49 per cent of most individuals who end a diet.

c. Have low self-esteem with meals. It's understandable that every diet program taught you never to trust the body or the food you dedicate. Although it may be the procedure for the diet that fails, failure continues to undermine its romantic relationship with food.

d. Since you don't deserve to consume because you're overweight.

e. Reduced duration of the diet. Living on a diet is getting shorter. (It could be indisputable that the Ultra Slim-Fast sales page is "Give us weekly ... and we ..."

f. Last dinner. All diet plans are preceded by foods that you presume not to eat anymore. Food consumption often increases during this period. It can happen with a meal or in a few days. The last supper seems to be the last step before the "nutritional cleansing", almost a farewell party. For a single customer, Marilyn, each meal seemed to be the last. I ate every meal until it filled up uncomfortable since I was terrified that I would never eat again. Once for all reasons! He was on a diet because the first grade exceeded two-thirds of his existence! He experienced provisional fasting intervals and a series of low-calorie diets. As for his body, the diets were just around the corner, so it's best to eat when you can. Any food for Marilyn was a relief from hunger.

g. Social abstinence. Since it is difficult to go on a diet and visit a party or go out for dinner, it is easier to refuse social invitations. At first, social avoidance of food may seem wiser for dieting reasons, but it becomes a big deal. There is often the concern of being able to maintain static control. It is not unusual for this meeting to be strengthened by "maintaining calorie intake or excess grams of fat for the party", which often means eating almost nothing. But by enough time the dieter finds the party, ravenous food cravings dominates and consuming feels very uncontrollable.

h. Sluggish metabolism. Each diet plan shows your body to adjust better to another purposeful starvation (another eating routine arrangement). The digestion backs off as the body utilizes each calorie successfully, as though it were the last. The more extreme the eating routine, the more it will push your body into the endurance condition that diminishes calories. Bolstering your digestion is like filling a fire. Expel the strong wood, and the fire diminishes. Essentially, to build the pace of digestion, we should eat a satisfactory measure of calories; generally, our life structures will redress and back off.

i. Use caffeine to endure the day. Espresso and diet drinks will, in general, be manhandled as a supervisory group to feel fiery while eating pretty much nothing.

j.   Eating disorder. At long last, for a few, the rehashed diet is generally the foundation of a dietary problem (going from anorexia nervosa or bulimia to impulsive indulging).

Despite the fact that Sandra felt she could never again follow dieting, she was as yet engaged with the most recent wonder of the Supper. (We frequently meet him each time we see somebody just because.) Truth be told, she ate higher nourishment levels than expected and ate huge numbers of her preferred nourishments (he figured he could never observe these kinds of nourishment again). It seems as though you are arranging a long outing and planning additional garments. The straightforward thought of concentrating on her eating issues put her in the attitude of the pre-diet plan, something normal.

While Sandra essentially started to comprehend the worthlessness of the dieting, she should be slim had not changed, obviously a predicament. She clung to the appeal of honourable American want.

The Paradox of Dieting

Inside our general public, the quest for slenderness (both for wellbeing and physical make-up) has wound up being the call to war of clearly all Americans. Eating an individual nibble of any nourishment that is high in fat or non-healthfully redeemable is generally deserving of a "blameworthy" expression by affiliation. You may be paroled, in any case, for "extraordinary conduct." Good conduct, inside our way of life, implies beginning a crisp eating routine or having incredible aims to abstain from food. Along these lines starts the hardship routine of dieting - the battle of the "bulge and indulge". Rice cakes for seven days, Häagen-Dazs the following.

"I feel remorseful essentially for enabling the staple worker to perceive what I purchase," said another client, who by chance had his trolley loaded with a natural product, vegetables, entire grains, pasta and a little 16 ounces of genuine dessert. It seems as though we were in a state of utilization of the Food Law coordinated by the nourishment mafia. Furthermore, there consistently is by all accounts dieting you can't refuse. Embellishment? No. We are sensible for this discernment.

A report distributed in 1993 in Eating Disorders-The Journal of Treatment and Avoidance found that somewhere in the range of 1973 and 1991, notices for dietary guides (diet nourishments, nourishment decrease helps, and diet programs) expanded practically direct. The analysts likewise referenced that there is absolutely a parallel model at the beginning of utilization issue. It is speculated that the weight of the push on the dietary arrangement (through publicizing spots) for the most part importantly affects the pattern of buyer unsettling influence.

The dieting pressure plan is powered past TV ads. Magazine articles and film content add to the weight of being thin. Fragile cigarette announcements additionally go for the heaviness of the Achilles female heel with titles like Ultra Thin 100, Virginia Slims, and so forth. A Kent cigarette, "Thin Lights", explicitly portrays this push on ladies' physical issues. Your promotion is like that of an industrialist for a decrease in normal weight contrasted with a cigarette, featuring lean depictions: "long", "slight", "light". Obviously, the examples in cigarette ads are especially unpretentious. Obviously, the inside for disease control (CDC) traits and expansion in ladies' smoking to their need to be more slender. Tragically, we have heard ladies ponder in our workplaces who have likewise viewed as smoking again as a guide to getting more fit.

Be that as it may, weight reduction isn't only a worry of ladies (albeit clearly there is extra weight on ladies). The multiplication of business contributions of light lager has planted the seed of body mindfulness in men's considerations; in addition, a fit stomach is desirable over one of brew. It is no occurrence that we have seen the dispatch of magazines focused on men, for example, Males Fitness and Female's Health.

While the quest for slenderness has crossed the sexual orientation boundary, we have sadly brought forth the original of weight onlookers — an upsetting pattern towards new dieting influences the wellness of American youngsters. Stunning exploration has shown that school-age kids are fixating on their weight-an impression of a nation eager about dieting and overabundance weight. The nation over, six-year-olds are getting thinner, scared of putting on weight, and being continuously treated for utilization issue that compromises their wellbeing and development protection. Social strain to shed pounds has bombed in kids.

Not exclusively can eating less junk food work; it is generally the principle issue. Albeit many may follow dieting as a push to lose abundance weight or for wellbeing reasons, the conundrum is clearly that it could cause more damage. This is the thing that our nation must show to the eating routine:

a. Obesity is greater than any time in recent memory in grown-ups and youngsters.

b. Dietary problems are on the ascent.

c. Child weight issues have multiplied in the previous ten years.

d. Despite the way that there are still more without fat and dietary nourishments than previously, just about 66% of grown-ups are hefty or fat.

e. More than one thousand 200 and a lot of fat has just been liposuction from 1982 to 1992. (And as of late accessible review indicated that once a year after a liposuction procedure, fat returned, yet in another area of the body).

f. Diet builds the possibility to increase significantly a greater number of pounds than you have lost!

Dieting Intake Cannot Battle Biology

Diet is a kind of transient yearning. Accordingly, when you are given a principal chance to eat truly, you experience so firmly that you feel wild, an edgy demonstration. With respect to natural yearning, all expectations to design the eating routine and the need to get in shape are temporary and incomprehensibly superfluous. In those concise minutes, we become simply like the voracious man-expending plant in the film Little Store of Horrors, testing to eat-"Feed me, feed me."

While outrageous eating may appear to be crazy and unnatural, it is really a standard reaction to yearning and diet. Notwithstanding, it can frequently be viewed as that eating after the dieting doesn't have "determination" or imperfection in character. Be that as it may, in translating the post-dietary nourishment plan accordingly, it gradually disintegrates fearlessness with nourishment, diet after eating routine. Each infringement of the eating routine arrangement, each nourishment situation that appears to be wild establishes the frameworks for the "diet plan mindset", step by step and diet by diet. The evidently daring arrangement invest more energy following time-transforms into as dumbfounding as the Chinese finger confound. You can't fight science. At the point when your body starves, it should be bolstered. In any case, frequently a weight watcher gripes: "Just on the off chance that I experience determination." Clearly, this isn't just a self-control issue. (In spite of the fact that the splendid tribute from fat misfortune treatment focuses support this lost blame in determination.) When you are not encouraged, you will get fixated on nourishment, regardless of whether on a purposeful eating routine or craving.

You can't count calories, yet eat cautiously for the sake of wellbeing. This is by all accounts the politically right term for "diet" during the 90s. Be that as it may, in any event, for some, it's a similar issue with dinners, with similar side effects. Keeping away from overabundance fats or sugars, whatever occurs, and subsisting on basically sans fat or starch-free nourishments is basically an eating routine and frequently brings about a lacking eating routine. There are numerous kinds of diets and different sorts of diets. We will investigate your dietary character and meet the Intuitive Eater in the following part.

Diet Increases your Risk of Getting More Weight!

On the off chance that dietary applications were to withstand a similar control as medications, open utilization probably won't be permitted. Envision, for instance, taking asthma to medicate, which improves relaxing for half a month; however, over the long haul; it exacerbates the lungs and relaxing. Will I truly follow an eating routine (a great supposed "reasonable eating routine"), in the event that I realized I could make you put on weight?

Here is a couple of calming research demonstrating that eating less junk food advances weight gain:

a. A gathering of UCLA specialists inspected thirty-one long haul investigated on eating less junk food and figured slimming down is a consistent indicator of overabundance weight gain-up to 66% of the individuals recovered more abundance weight than they dropped (Mann et al., 2007).

b. Research on almost seventeen thousand kids between the ages of nine and fourteen finished up: "... in the long haul, the weight-controlling eating routine isn't just ineffectual, yet could advance weight gain" (Field et al. 2003).

c. People on a high school diet had twice the same number of odds of being overweight than adolescents on dieting regarding a multiyear review. Specifically, toward the start of the examination, individuals on an eating routine don't gauge significantly more than their companions who don't follow dieting. This is a significant detail, provided that individuals on dieting weigh much more, it could be a component of perplexity (which would suggest extra factors, as opposed to counting calories, for example, genetics).

Epic research on more than 2,000 units of twins from Finland, matured 16 to 25 years matured indicated that consuming fewer calories itself, free of hereditary qualities, is impressively connected with quickened fat addition and expanded danger of getting stout (Pietilaineet et al. 2011). Dietary twins, who experienced a solitary purposeful health improvement plan, were just about a few times bound to be overweight than their non-dietary twin partner. Likewise, the plausibility of unreasonable overweight improved in a portion subordinate way with every dietary occasion.

Studies aside: what did your dietary experiences show you? Numerous people and individuals in the lab state their first dieting plan was straightforward: the pounds basically liquefied away. Yet, that first dietary experience could be the temptation trap, which starts the vain quest for weight decrease through eating routine. We state pointless on the grounds that our bodies are amazingly wise and designed for endurance.

Organically, your body experiences the dieting process predominantly in light of the fact that it is a sort of starvation. Your cells don't comprehend you are intentionally limiting your dinner admission. The body shifts into base endurance mode-digestion diminish, and nourishment needing heighten. What's more, with each diet plan, your body learns and adjusts, which prompts weight gain in expansion. Therefore, many people feel simply like they absolutely are a disappointment; however, it truly is eating less junk food which has bombed them.

CHAPTER 2:

What Type of Eater Are You?

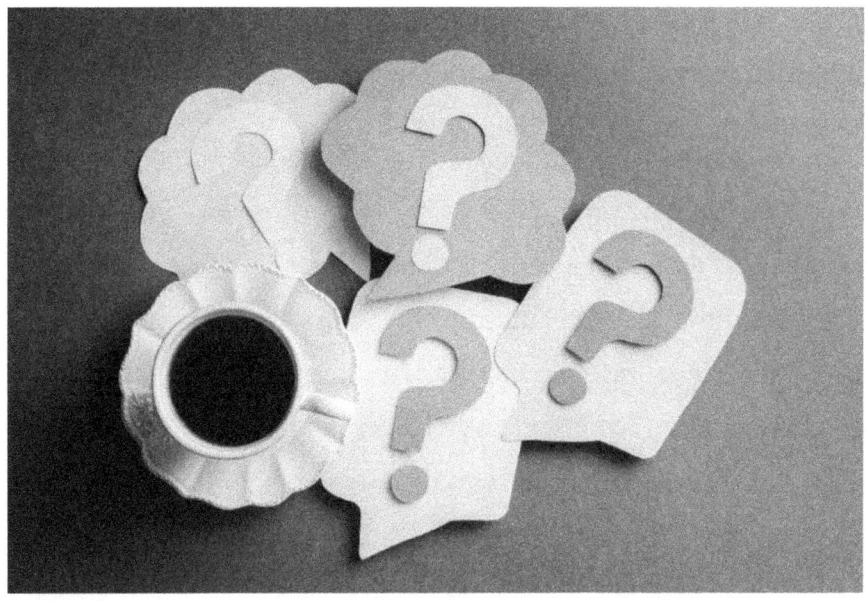

Y ou can continue on a diet and not know! There are many types of eating styles that are actually unconscious types of dieting. Quite a few people have said these were not really on a diet plan- but upon nearer inspection of what and how they consume, they were dieting still!

A good example here's. Ted arrived because he wished to lose excess weight. He said that in his fifty years of life, he had previously only been on four serious diet programs. In examining the titles of publications at work (compulsory overeating texts, consumption of books on ailments, etc.), he said: "You use many serious complications in the diet ... well, I'm not just one of those. Obviously, Ted did not consider himself a dietician, who ate simply with care, but showed that it was an unconscious diet.

Although Ted had not followed an active diet, he was eating at a level where he had almost passed out in the afternoon. The reason: he had been unhappy with his weight! In the morning I chose an intense bicycle trip down a hill, for only an hour. I would go back and have breakfast for a bit. Lunch was usually a salad with iced tea (although it seems healthy, it is too low in carbohydrates). At dinner time, your body will scream for meals. Ted not only had a severe calorie deficit, but he also lacked carbohydrates. Nights become a food party! Ted had the idea that it was previously a "food volume" problem with a solid sweet tooth. The truth is that previously he had an unconscious mentality in the diet that biologically triggered his night diet and his pleasant tooth.

Even Alicia hadn't been on a conscious diet. She never came to lose pounds, but because she wanted to increase her vitality. During the initial program, it became clear that he had problems with food. So they asked him if he had done many diets. She seemed amazed. "How did you know I did billions of diets?" While Alicia claimed to be comfortable with her current fat, she was still at war with food; she did not trust herself with meals. It turns out that Alicia has been on a diet since she was a child. Although he hadn't officially followed a diet, he maintained (and expanded) a couple of dietary guidelines with each diet plan that almost paralyzed her ability to eat normally. We observe this at all times, the hangover from dieting: avoiding certain foods no matter what, feeling uncontrollable as soon as a "sinful" meals are eaten, sense guilty when self-imposed food guidelines are broken (such as for example "Thou shalt not really eat previous to 6 P.M."), and so forth.

The unconscious diet usually occurs in the type of meticulous eating habits. There can be an excellent line between feeding on for health insurance and dieting. Notice how actually the frozen diet plan foods such as for example, Lean Cuisine and Excess weight Watchers are placing their focus on health instead of a diet. As long as you participate in some form of the diet, the recipient will eliminate food and body concerns. Whether you are a conscious or unconscious person, the results of the medial side are similar, the diet again, the effect of the eyelashes. It seems like a period in which one eats cautiously, "blowing" it and spending penance with an increase in diet or extremely cautious consumption. In this chapter, we will explore the many diet/nutrition styles to help see what your position is now. Later, you will meet the Intuitive Eater and the intuitive style of food, and the perfect solution is to live without diet programs.

The Eating Personalities

To help you clarify your food design style (or diet), we have identified the following key types of eaters that feature distinctive food patterns: the careful eater, the one that makes a professional diet and the eater unconscious. These consuming personalities are exhibited even if they are not officially on a diet. It is possible to have significantly more than one consuming personality, although we find that there is commonly a dominant trait. The chances of your life can also influence or change your personality to eat. For example, a client, a tax attorney, was usually a careful eater, but during the fiscal period of the year, it became the chaotic unconscious eater.

It is possible that it occasionally possesses the intake characteristics described below in the three nuclei that feed on personality. Note this, and if your feed exists in one of these domains most of the time, it's a problem.

Review each character you eat and see which one best reflects your style. By understanding what your position is now, it will be easier to find out how to become an intuitive eater. For example, you may find that you have already been involved in a type of diet and have not even recognized it. Or you can discover features that, without knowing it, work against you.

The careful eater

Cautious consumers are those who tend to be attentive to the food they put into their bodies. Ted was a good example of a careful eater (per day). At the top, accurate eaters look like "ideal" eaters. They are highly aware of nutrition. Externally, they seem oriented towards health and fitness (noble characteristics admired and strengthened in our society).

Style

There is a selection of eating behaviours exhibited by Careful Eater. In an intense moment, Cautious Eater can be distressed for every bite of food allowed in the body. Shopping trips are spent looking at meal labels. Eating out can indicate interrogating the waiter what's in the meals, how maybe the meals prepared-and obtaining assurances that the meals are prepared particularly to the Cautious Eater's liking (not often one speck of essential oil or other excess fat used). What's incorrect with this? Aren't label reading and assertive cafe ordering in the medical interests of some individuals? Of program! However, the difference could be the vigilante force and the ability to forget any defect related to the choice of consumption. Attentive eaters tend to consume less than normal and control the amount of food consumed.

The attentive eater can spend most of his waking hours planning another meal or snack, often worried about eating. Since Careful Eater is not officially on a diet, your brain punishes all the "harmful", fatty or sugary foods you eat. The Careful Eater can travel the fine line between sincerely thinking about health and eating carefully with respect to body image. Sometimes, Careful Eater is driven by periods or events. For example, some careful eaters are meticulous during weekdays, to make sure they get their "ideal of consumption" to "show off" on the weekends or for the next party. But on weekends they happen 104 times a year: waste can be counterproductive with unwanted weight gain. Consequently, it is not uncommon for a cautious eater to think about starting a diet.

The Problem

There's nothing incorrect with being thinking about the well -being of the body. However, the problem occurs when diligent consumption (almost in contact with the militant) affects a healthy relationship with food and negatively affects the body. Prudent eaters, on closer inspection, resemble a delicate diet style. They can't be on a diet; however, they look into every food scenario.

The Professional Dieter

People on a professional diet are easier to identify; they are on a perpetual diet. In general, they tried the latest commercial diet, the diet book or the trick to lose weight. Sometimes, the diet is performed in the form of fasting or "reduction". Professional Dieters understand a whole lot about portions of foods, calories, and "dieting methods," yet the cause they are usually on another diet plan is that the initial one never worked. Today, Professional Dieter can be amply trained in counting carbohydrate grams.

Style

People on a professional diet also have accurate food traits. The difference, however, is that people on a diet chronically, guiding the choice of meals to lose weight, not necessarily for health. When the dieter is not officially on a diet, he generally thinks about the next diet that can be started. He often wakes up wishing this is a good day, the fresh start. While people on a professional diet have a lot of knowledge of diets, they don't serve them well. It is not uncommon to allow them to eat compulsively or participate in the consumption of the Last Supper as soon as a prohibited meal is eaten. This is because people on a chronic diet really believe that they will no longer eat this food; tomorrow I'm on a diet, tomorrow they start again with a clean slate. Better eat right now; it's the last opportunity. And in addition, the Professional Dieter gets discouraged at the futility of the vicious routine. Diet, lose weight, put on weight, intermittent binges, and back again to dieting.

The Problem

It's very difficult to live in this manner. The Yo-Yo diet helps make losing excess weight more difficult as well as eating healthy. Chronic lack of food usually causes overeating or periodic feeding. For some diet professionals, the frustration of losing weight intensifies so much that they can try laxatives, diuretics and weight loss supplements. And trigger that these "dietary aids" generally don't work, they could try extreme methods like chronic restriction, in the type of anorexia nervosa or bleeding (like nausea after a binge), in the type of bulimia. While anorexia and bulimia are multifactorial and have their roots in psychological problems, a growing body of research suggests that chronic diet is usually a common step towards an eating disorder. One study specifically found that when enough dieters reach the age of fifteen, they are eight times more likely to have problems with an eating disorder than people who don't go on a diet.

The Unconscious Eater

The Unconscious Eater is often engaged in a paired diet, which consists of eating and simultaneously doing another activity, such as watching television and eating, or eating and reading. Due to the subtleties and insufficient awareness, it can become problematic for a person to recognize this eating character. There are numerous subtypes of unconscious eaters.

The Chaotic Unconscious Eater

Live a life that is too often programmed, too busy, too many things you can do. The chaotic, consuming design is haphazard; whatever's obtainable will end up being grabbed -vending machine fare, junk food, it'll all perform. Food and diet tend to be vital to this person-just not really in the critical instant of the chaos. Chaotic eaters tend to be so busy putting out fires that have difficulty identifying biological cravings for food until it is fiercely voracious. And in addition, the chaotic eater will go extended periods of time without eating.

The Refuse-Not Unconscious Eater

They are vulnerable to the simple existence of food, regardless of whether they are hungry or full. The jars of sweets, the meals at the meetings, the food sitting on the kitchen counter, probably none of them will be overcome. However, most of the time, it is fair; consumers who do not refuse to consume are not aware of what they are consuming or how much they consume. For example, the Reject-Not Eater can actually pick up some candy on the way to the bathroom without being aware of it. Social outings that revolve around meals such as cocktails and festive buffets are particularly difficult for Refuse-Not Eater.

The Waste-Not Unconscious Eater

Evaluate meals in dollars. His / her eating travel is frequently influenced by getting just as much as they are able to your money can buy. Waste-Not Eater is particularly inclined to completely clean the plate (and also that of others). It is not unusual for a waste eater not to actually consume the leftovers of children or spouse.

The Unconscious Emotional Eater

They use food to manage emotions, especially unpleasant feelings such as stress, anger and loneliness. While Emotional Eaters look at their consuming as the problem, it's often a sign of a deeper concern. Consuming behaviours of the Emotional Eater can range between grabbing a bag of chips on stressful occasions to chronic compulsive binges of huge quantities of food.

The problem

Unconscious power, in its many forms, usually be a problem if it translates into persistent excessive consumption (which can simply occur if you are eating instead of being very alert). Remember that somewhere between the first and last bite of meals is where the awareness period actually occurs. Like in "Oh, it's all over!"

For example, have you ever bought a large package of candy in the movies and started consuming it, and then you find that your fingertips suddenly scratch themselves under the empty container?

This is a simple type of unconscious feeding. But unconscious nutrition can also exist at an extreme level, in a relatively altered feeding condition. In this case, the individual is not attentive to what is consumed, why he has started eating, or how he knows about the taste of the food. That is zoning out with meals.

When your Eating Personality Works Against You

Finally, the food varieties of Careful Eater, Professional Dieter and Unconscious Eater become an inefficient feeding method, even if at the top they seem to be fine. The perfect solution is for the discouraged consumer: try more with a fresh diet!

At first, the new diet seems stimulating and hopeful, but in the end, the family pounds return. The diet becomes more demanding, and even if you resume your basal consumption personality, you may feel more unpleasant than before. It is because internal dietary guidelines are strengthened with each diet plan. T hese meal rules often perpetuate the guilt emotions of consumption, even when you are not officially on a diet. Furthermore, the biological ramifications of the diet make it increasingly difficult to have a normal romantic relationship with meals. The Intuitive Eater character, however, can be an exception. It's the only feeding design that doesn't work against you and will help you end chronic diets and yo-yo weight fluctuations.

Intuitive Eater Introduction

Intuitive eaters march with their signs of internal hunger and eat regardless of what they choose without feeling guilty or an ethical dilemma. The intuitive eater can be an independent eater. However, it is increasingly difficult to become an unaltered eater in today's health-conscious society considering the bombardment of communications on food, food and weight by advertisers, the press and medical researchers. When we explained the basic feeding characteristics of Intuitive Eater to its customers, it is surprising how often we will hear the answer: "This is how my partner eats." This or how my boyfriend eats. "When we ask what the person's weight and romantic relationship is with food, the answer is: "No problem!" Consider small children. Intuitive, natural eaters will be practically free of social messages about meals and body image. Toddlers possess innate wisdom of meals, in the event that you don't hinder it. They don't eat predicated on dieting guidelines or health, yet study after research shows that if you allow a toddler consumes spontaneously; he'll eat what he requirements when given free usage of food. (This is most likely the toughest point for a concerned mother or father to do- to release and trust that children have an innate capability to eat!)

This is true even when food for food, food for little tykes is apparently a father's nightmare. Experts found that calorie intake was highly variable in confirmed foods; However, it has been balanced over time. However, many parents assume that their children cannot properly regulate their diet.

As a result, parents often adopt coercive strategies in an attempt to ensure that the child eats a nutritionally sufficient diet. But a previous study by Birch and his colleagues indicates that these control strategies are countered. In addition, Birch notes that "parents' attempts to regulate their children's feeding have been reported more regularly by obese adults than by normal-weight adults." Likewise, Duke University psychologist Philip Costanzo,

PhD found that unwanted weight in school-age children was closely related to the level at which parents sought to limit their children's food. Actually, well-meaning parents hinder Intuitive Eating. Whenever a mother or father attempts to overrule a child's organic eating cues, the nagging problem gets worse, not better.

A parent, who feeds a kid every time a hunger signal is heard and who stops feeding when the infant demonstrates he's had enough, may play a robust role in the original development of Intuitive Feeding on. Indeed, the innovative role of the therapist and dietician offered by Ellyn Satter has shown that, in the event that the parents of obese children cool down and allow them to consume without the pressure of their parents, the children will ultimately eat much less. Why? The child begins to listen and understand his internal signs of hunger and satiety. The child also knows that he will use food.

According to Satter, "children deprived of food so that they can lose weight, worry about food, fear they don't have enough to eat and are susceptible to overeating if they get the chance." We have found that this is accurate for dieters too. Limited to adults, the intuitive drinking process has been buried over a long period, often years and years.

Instead of relaxing a father's pressure, this decrease in pressure should be the result of inside and against the myth of society about dieting and distorted body worship.

Fortunately, we all have the natural ability to eat intuitively; It has simply been suppressed, especially with the diet. This book specializes in showing you exactly how to wake the intuitive eater in you.

How Your Intuitive Eater Gets Buried

As toddlers get yourself a little older, the mixed messages start to creep in-from the early influences of the Saturday morning food commercial, to the well-meaning mother or father who coaxes his kid to "Clean your plate." The assault won't stop if you're a kid. There are many external forces that impact our eating, that may include additionally bury Intuitive Eating.

Dieting

You have already seen the damage from a chronic diet, which includes, among others:

a. Increase in excessive consumption
b. Decreased metabolic rate.
c. Greater concern about meals.
d. Increase the emotions of deprivation.
e. A greater sense of failure
f. Reduced feeling of willpower.

This only serves to erode your confidence in food and prompts you to rely on external sources to guide your diet (one diet, one diet and enough time of the day, food rules, etc.). The more you head to external resources to "judge" if your consuming is in balance, the additional removed you feel from Intuitive Eating. Intuitive Eating depends on your inner cues and signals.

Eat Healthy Messages Or Die

Messages about healthy eating are everywhere, from nonprofit healthcare organizations to food companies promoting the medical benefits of their unique item. The inherent message? Everything you consume can improve your wellbeing. Conversely, take one incorrect move (bite), and you're one step nearer to the grave. Is usually this an exaggeration? No. For example, a 1994 press release published by the Harvard College of Public Health mentioned that the consumption of trans-fatty acids (inside margarine) could cause thirty thousand deaths each year in the United States due to cardiovascular disease. That sort of message can easily keep you feeling guilty for consuming the "incorrect" kind of meals and feeling puzzled in what you should eat.

Magazines and newspapers have also significantly increased their protection of food and well-being. A food publisher, Joe Crea, of an important metropolitan newspaper, the Orange County Register (California), said that in a period of six to 12 months (1987-1993) his stories about food multiplied by five. Of nearly eight hundred food stories, two hundred had been linked to health problems. Although there is absolutely no doubt that everything you eat can affect your health, exponential coverage of the press has been offered as a channel for the development of food paranoia in the purchaser, particularly in the diet. Joe Crea agrees: "Open the newspaper, visit a good story about cheesecake and, at the same time, another piece on how eating too much will make you gain weight. Place the incompatible player. Are we saying you should ignore the virtues of healthy intake? Of course not. However, if you have a diet adapted to your diet, the burst of "healthy eating" messages can make you feel more guilty about the foods you choose to eat. Obesity and Wellness reported a study of 2,075 adults in Florida that revealed that 45% of adults felt guilty after eating the foods they liked. (Remember that this study was carried out to reflect common American demographics. These "guilt-by- eating" figures would probably be higher if performed on dieters.) Women could be particularly guilty. A Gallup poll by the American Dietetic Association showed that women feel more guilty than men for the foods they eat (44 per cent versus 28 per cent). Could this be because females diet more often than men? Or because ladies are usually the prospective of health communications and food advertisements (consider the number of women's magazines). Women will be primarily responsible for decisions relating to family health care and will often also be responsible for food and nutritional problems; They serve as the main objective.

We have found that establishing a healthy diet or diet as a short priority in the intuitive feeding process is counterproductive. We initially ignore nutrition, as it interferes with the relearn process of an intuitive eater.

Nutrition heresy? No. Food can be respected and honoured. It simply cannot be the first priority when you've been on a diet for a lifetime. Or consider it this way; in case you have focused all your attention on the diet, does it help you? The many nutritious diet programs (absolute) may become embraced as another type of diet.

CHAPTER 3:

Intuitive Eating Standards: Summary

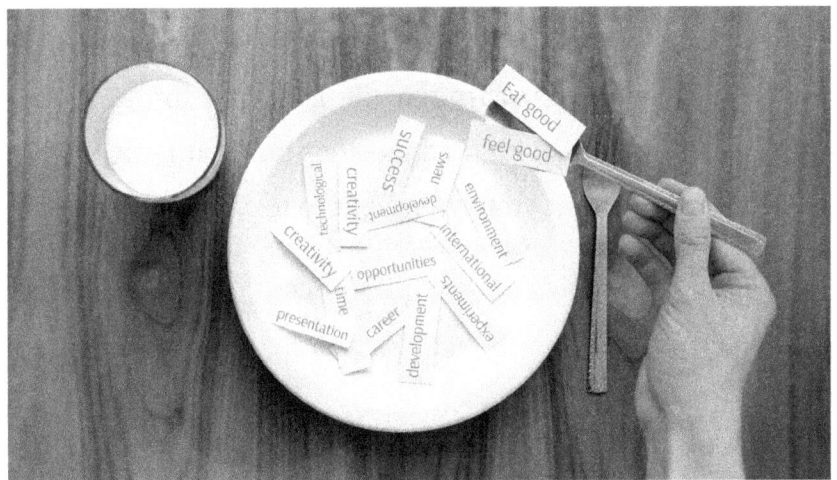

J ust once he vows to dispose of the diet and supplant it with an activity focused on intuitive nourishing, is he considering escaping jail from abundance weight variances and food fixations? In this part, we will present the fundamental ideas of intuitive sustaining: a preview of every idea, with an examination study or two. The most significant aftereffect of every customer referenced was that of acquiring a sound association with dinners and their bodies. By following ten intuitive eating ideas, you will standardize your sentimental association with food. A focus on weight reduction must be set aside for later. On the off chance that your present pounds offer came about because of getting withdrawn together with your inward insight about eating, and subsequently, of tuning back into this intelligence, weight reduction happens, along these lines be it. Assuming, by the by, you are as of now keeping your set point fat through the action of limiting, overeating, confining, and so forth, at that point, it truly is particularly essential that you put weight to decrease on the storage compartment burner.

Guideline One:

Declines the Mentality of the Dietary Plan

Dispense with diet books and magazine articles that give you the bogus any desire for getting more fit rapidly, effectively and for all time. Feel furious about the falsehoods that made you sense that you had flopped each time a new diet quit working and you recovered all your weight. On the off chance that you enable a little want to demand that a crisp and better diet might be hiding close by, it will keep you from abstaining from rediscovering the intuitive diet.

For quite a while, we have sought after one diet plan for another, enabling the most stylish trend to direct what, how much, and when to eat. This inflexible way of life of limitation and hardship can bring about a dangerous association with food. The initial step on the intuitive sustenance scale is, for the most part, to depend on your impulses with respect to food decisions.

Guideline Two:

Respect Your Hunger

Keep your body organically encouraged with adequate vitality and sugars. Else you can bring about base travel to indulge. When you reach the top appetite, all aims of moderate, conscious eating are passing and unessential. Seeing how to respect this first organic sign units the phase for revamping trust with yourself and dinners.

While most diets need you to object to a growling stomach, intuitive nutrition renews your body's signals. You'll make sense of how to be increasingly aware of your food yearnings and how precisely to react appropriately to it before you feel hungry. Attempt this in the home: Before each dinner, rate your level of yearning, record a couple of internal signals that you saw, and enough time of day. Do this for week by week, and you'll are more in order together with your hunger, and furthermore which foods convey dependable vitality and the ones that are quickly catching fire and convey short-lived satiety.

Guideline Three:

MAKE PEACE WITH FOOD

Call a détente; quit the food battle! Give unconditional approval to food. In the event that you illuminate yourself that you can't or shouldn't have a particular food, it can bring about serious feelings of hardship that incorporate with wild longings and, regularly, gorging. At the point when you at last "give up" to your illegal foods, eating will be acquainted with such force, it, for the most part, results in Last Supper overeating and overpowering blame.

Intuitive eating solicits that you forsake the idea from awful and the great food. That system energizes an unsafe 'win big or bust by any stretch of the imagination' attitude that may bring about longings for 'taboo' foods, joined by gorging and a rush of self-hatred and disgrace. Intuitive eating advances the hypothesis that food ought to be viewed as an actual existence upgrading experience.

Guideline Four:

Challenge The Meals Police

Shout a boisterous "basically no" to contemplations in your mind that proclaim you're "extraordinary" for eating under one thousand calories or "horrendous" in light of the fact that you ate a touch of chocolate cake. THE MEALS LAW AUTHORIZATIONS POLICE, the nonsensical rules that dieting has created. The police headquarters is certainly housed somewhere down in your mind, and its own amplifier yells ominous points, sad expressions, and blame inciting arraignments. Pursuing the suppers Police aside is a significant advance in time for Intuitive Eating. An escalated mental housekeeping and reframing disposition toward suppers are pivotal. Watch any food law authorization considerations you may have, such as "I was poor today" or "I shouldn't eat that." Resist the possibility that your food alternatives characterize it and the value it brings to the world. Pay special mind to people who might be deliberately or unwittingly showing a food police mindset, at that point talk about your intuitive eating way of thinking with them and have them to help you by hushing up about their terrible remarks.

Guideline Five:

Feel Your Fullness

Tune in for the body flags that let you realize that you are not any hungrier. Pay heed to the signs that show that you're effectively full. Interruption in the focal point of suppers or nibble and have yourself the manner in which the food tastes, and what your present completion level is.

The other side of regarding your appetite is to regard when you're full. Since diet programs limit what, when, and exactly the amount you expend, it's easy to get detached from the internal signs that transmission satiety. At the point when you practice intuitive expending you take up a feast with a lesser degree of food yearnings and in a mentality which enables you to turn out to be increasingly fragile to prompts that you're full. In addition, you comprehend that you could refuel at whatever point you're ravenous once more, and you won't encounter constrained to clean your plate totally. Evaluate this at home: Make utilization of a satiety scale all through suppers to prepare your brain to address signs of satiety. Record perceptions of how you are feeling and all that you ate. This can help decide when to leave the fork and let the dinners actually feel supported and empowered.

Guideline Six:

Reveal The Satisfaction Factor

JAPAN has the knowledge to keep joy as you of their objectives of sound living. Inside our anger to be thin and sound, we regularly ignore likely the essential presents of presence the happiness and fulfilment, which can be inside the eating experience. At the point when you take in what you need, in a domain that is welcoming, the fulfilment you infer is incredible power in helping you are feeling fulfilled and content. By giving this experience to yourself, you will see that it takes essentially less food to pick; you've had "enough."

Intuitive eating urges you to perceive foods that really cause you to feel great all through supper, yet a short time later, as well. You will find yourself floating towards and time for the foods that produce you feel your absolute best. Besides to relishing suppers and eating groceries that taste extraordinary and make you feel incredible, you can connect the entirety of your faculties: slow down, acknowledge what kind of food looks, regard how it achieved your plate, inhale every one of the fragrances, and eat inside a domain that appears to be acceptable expedite the plants and candles-and with people who light you up.

Guideline Seven:

Adapt Together To Your Emotions Without Needing Food

Discover approaches to solace and simplicity, sustain, occupy, and illuminate your passionate worries without utilizing food. Stress, depression, weariness, and outrage are sentiments a large portion of us experience all through presence. Everyone has its trigger, and every offer its own conciliation. Suppers won't fix these sentiments. It could comfort for the present moment, divert from the distress, or really numb you directly into a food aftereffect. However, food won't solve the problem. In the event that anything, eating for an enthusiastic yearning is just going to make you feel more awful after some time. You'll, in the end, need to adapt to the wellspring of the feeling, alongside the distress of overeating. Indeed, food could be encouraging, yet that delight just keeps going insofar as the food. A short time later, anything that was eating you stays, covered under food, perhaps now offered with a piece of blame and disgrace. Intuitive eating urges you to perceive whether you're sense on edge, exhausted, desolate, tragic, or irate and look for a veritable arrangement. Get a walk, call a dear companion, practice reflection or yoga, get a remedial back rub, read a composed book, or make in a diary. You'll comprehend you're reacting appropriately when the reaction empowers you to feel good, not more terrible.

Guideline Eight:

Respect Your Body

Acknowledge your hereditary outline. Just for the most part in light of the fact that an individual with a footwear size of eight wouldn't ordinarily foresee reasonably to crush directly into a size six, it truly is correspondingly useless (and horrendous) to have a comparable desire regarding the matter of body size. Regard the body, so you can encounter better about who you are. It's difficult to dismiss the dietary plan attitude in the event that you are ridiculous and excessively pivotal of the body shape. Our varieties are our superpowers, but we live in a world that idealizes a cut body type. The possibility that individuals can profoundly change our life structures is typically unreasonable and ridiculous. Intuitive eating troubles you to grasp your hereditary plan set handy expectations, and praise your uniqueness. Evaluate this in the home: Anytime you catch yourself contrasting the body with someone else's, react as you'll if a buddy said something practically identical regarding themselves.

Guideline Nine:

Exercise-Feel The Difference

Disregard activist exercise. Just get dynamic and experience the distinction. Move your concentrate to how it appears to go your body, as opposed to the fat consuming limit impact of the activity. On the off chance that you focus on how you are feeling from working out, such as empowered, it could have the effect between turning up for an energetic morning hour's walk and striking the rest caution. If when you stirred, your solitary target is to lose abundance weight, rarely do you get an inspiring component at that time of period. People who practice intuitive benefiting from appreciating practice since it gives them vitality improves their inclination, advances self-adequacy, and makes them experience solid, adaptable, and dexterous. Preparing isn't about which movement will consume off the most calories, however rather about which action might be the best time and stimulating. It's another exemplary instance of the manner in which the fulfilment factor could make propensities stick. The exercise you appreciate is an exercise that you're bound to do it once more, creating the force that drives feasible, long haul bliss.

Guideline Ten:

Respect Your Healthy And Soft Food

Choose foods that respect your prosperity and taste buds while making you feel better. Comprehend that you don't have to eat a perfect diet to be invigorating. You won't all of a sudden get yourself a supplement lack, or put on weight in one bite, one food, or one day of eating. It's what you normally eat after some time that issues. Progress, not so much flawlessness, is what makes a difference. Recognizing how your prosperity impacts the wealth, you will ever have shallow known purposes behind health objectives and grounds your thought processes in what is important: your individual qualities. Getting the point of view on why health is significant can assist you with the understanding that no supper or chomp could represent the moment of truth your self-esteem. Adjust your prosperity to your aspirations, and you will be significantly progressively inspired to develop rehearses that help your day by day life objectives.

AN ACTIVITY WITH GREAT REWARDS

Numerous people have been disappointed with their association with food and their bodies. Many experienced endeavoured either formal or casual dieting and had encountered disappointment and gloom. By learning the ideas of Intuitive Consuming and putting them to work, many will find an extending of the evaluation of life and quality about eating. You can go as well!

INTUITIVE EATING

A REVOLUTIONARY 4-STEP PROGRAM, BASED ON 10 PRINCIPLES, THAT WORKS! HOW THOUSANDS OF PEOPLE, REWIRING THEIR MINDS, STUCK TO THEIR DIET AND HAVE LOST MORE THAN 125 POUNDS (PART 2)

By **Meredith Carney**

Foreword

This integrative function illuminates how reasoning, once regarded as a "purely logical" setting of thinking, is in fact, reliant on the non-rational processing of our anatomies.

Knowing a little about the mind can help to realize why we're born with the wisdom we have to become Intuitive Eaters. Additionally, it may help us to observe how we're in a position to live an Intuitive Consuming life, even while becoming bombarded by the endless options of organic and refined foods open to us every day and the relentless diet plan messages that abound.

Human beings are privileged to see a dynamic interplay of instinct, emotion, and the mind mediates idea, which interacts to orchestrate life, and so. Mindfulness and psychiatrist expert, Daniel Siegel, M.D., calls this technique "Mind-Sight." There are three parts of the brain accountable for this powerful integration.

The first region is named the reptilian brain, since when the first reptiles roamed the planet earth; they acted and responded by instinct exclusively. They didn't rationalize, or feel-they merely went for this. As life evolved, another degree of brain function developed, called the limbic mind, which mammals possess also. Emotions and interpersonal behaviours originate right here. In the human limbic brain, feelings are layered upon the instincts of the reptilian mind. The abilities from the reptilian mind are delivered to the human limbic brain, which serves to increase consciousness. Ultimately, the third key area of the mind evolved, known as the rational mind, or the neo-cortex. The sensible human brain integrates instincts and emotions from the additional two brain regions. The sensible brain will not control instincts-instead; it perceives the instinctual and feeling elements of our beings and displays upon them. The rational mind creates thoughts and vocabulary.

Intuitive Eating embraces most three elements of the human being brain. In toddlerhood and infancy, eating is instinctual mostly. As we get older, thoughts and feelings frequently play a part in our decisions about eating. As we frequently tell our clients, our bodies are not only composed of the tongue and the stomach but the mind also. We've often heard somebody say, "I believed that as an Intuitive Eater, I possibly could eat whatever I needed. So, now I consume whatever I'd like and in so far as I want, whenever

I think like it!" In fact, this comment distorts the premise of intuitive feeding. Yes, make peace with meals, and consume what pleases your palate. Yes, provide yourself with the freedom to consume unconditionally, and eat just as much as you need to fulfil the body. But eating once you experience it, without respect for food cravings and fullness may not be an extremely satisfying experience and can even cause physical pain. Attunement, together with your body's satiety cues is usually an important part of the process.

As an Intuitive Eater, you'll be honouring your brain, because it is a component of the body. As you feel the concepts of Intuitive Eating, you'll be storing info in the memory "files" that you produce and house in the human brain. When you are feeling hungry, you will have to pull up a number of these files, while deciding what things to consume. You will evaluate how starving you are feeling and then consider what foods might fulfil your hunger as well as your taste buds. You may actually go through a number of sensual imaginings of the flavour and texture and heat of different foods. You may open the file to reflect on past eating experiences also. You may inquire yourself whether your current eating choice spent some time working out for you personally when you've consumed it previously. Achieved it sustains you very long enough? Achieved it makes your bloodstream sugars crash? Did you finish up with indigestion? Or do you thoroughly benefit from the food and want it again? Your feelings may also come into play when you have the desire to eat. Might you become upset and so are craving foods to comfort and ease and soothe yourself? Or are you bored and considering feeding on as a distraction? Considering these options might inform your decision about what things to eat, or even whether to consume/eat at all.

Initially of your trip to reclaim your Intuitive Eater, you will likely be hyperconscious of hunger, fullness, satisfaction, thoughts, and emotions. The human brain should be extremely in tune together with your tongue as well as your stomach. As you become even more adept at recognizing your internal signals, you might find that your instincts and intuitive wisdom consider even more of a prominent part in your eating encounter. Therefore, Intuitive Eating is actually about trusting you will be capable of accessing all the information you must have, by using all the areas of your brain-your reptilian instincts, your limbic reference to your emotions, as well as your rational thoughts.

Through Intuitive Eating, we figure out how to trust the wisdom which has always been within but has been blunted by years of self-doubt. Doubting their innate consuming signals had prolonged to doubting their beliefs about a great many other areas of their lives.

We've heard stories about individuals who have left abusive associations, made peace with estranged family members, and also have made significant profession changes, once they have a problem with meals and body has been resolved. We have also found out about new romances that, for a few, could not have already been possible while these were occupied with body issues and focused on the most recent doomed diet plan attempt. Intuitive Eating offers freed most of these people to continue with their lives while departing behind self-question and despair.

Introduction

If you could profit every diet just like a frequent flyer program, the majority of us could have earned a vacation to the moon and back. The almost $60 billion at 12 months, the weight-loss industry could finance the trip for generations to arrive (Bacon and Aphramor 2011). Ironically, we appear to have significantly more respect for our vehicles than for ourselves. If you took your vehicle to a car mechanic for regular tune-ups, and after money and time spent, the automobile didn't function, and you wouldn't blame yourself. Yet, regardless of the fact that 90 to 95 per cent of most diets fail-you have a tendency to blame yourself, not the dietary plan! Isn't it ironic that with an enormous failure price for dieting-we don't blame the procedure of dieting?

Initially, whenever we ventured into the globe of private practice, we didn't know each other. Yet, separately, each folk had remarkably similar guidance experiences that triggered us to rethink how exactly we work. This resulted in a significant change in how exactly we practice and years, later on, was the impetus because of this book.

My objective for Intuitive eating wasn't fame or fortune, however. When I sat right down to write the book, I simply wished to educate and motivate visitors to achieve superior health, whether they wished to lose weight, feel good, or invert a chronic disease. I experienced no idea the publication would take off, or that it could resonate so deeply with people all over the world. It seemed everyone began using that phrase-intuitive eating-to explain the overwhelmingly effective eating design detailed in reserve. And to this full-day, there are apparently never-ending blasts of discussions, describing miraculous health adjustments, caused by this topic.

The trick behind Intuitive eating's popularity is easy: It didn't promise an instant fix. Unlike crash diets that guarantee easy and instant results, "Intuitive eating" organized vital details about food and healthful eating that allowed visitors to be specialists in nutrition. The publication essentially paid to its visitors the keys to effective weight reduction so that these were in charge of their health destiny.

Center to Intuitive eating is a straightforward health equation, the core idea of my nutritarian program:

H = N / C Wellness = Nutrients / Calories

Your wellbeing is predicted by your nutrient intake divided by your calorie consumption.

I contact this core idea the nutrient density of your daily diet. Food gives us nutrition and calorie consumption (energy). All calories result from only three components: carbohydrates, fat, and proteins. Nutrients, however, come from noncaloric food factors, namely, vitamin supplements, nutrients, fibres, and phytochemicals, actually chemical substances that generally occur in plants. These noncaloric nutrients are quite crucial to your wellbeing. When the ratio of nutrition to calorie consumption is high, fat burns up, and wellness is restored. The even more nutrient-dense meals you consume, the, even more, you'll be happy with fewer calories, and the much less you'll crave excess fat and high-calorie foods.

A high-nutrient diet decreases growing older, helps restoration cells, reduces inflammation, and helps rid your body of toxins. High-nutrient, low-calorie foods include a great deal of dietary fibre and take up a whole lot of space in the stomach. As you consume a more substantial quantity of food, it satiates your food cravings and blunts your hunger.

Meeting the body's micronutrient requirements also helps suppress food craving and what I contact "toxic hunger, " which drives you to consume more calories than you require -usually in the type of processed foods, which can result in cancer and heart disease, among a great many other ailments.

Witnessing how Intuitive consuming inspired a lot of people to improve their diets not merely reinforced my results that high-nutrient diets create good wellness; it offered a considerable, ongoing body of proof proving that approach works. Nothing displays the energy of this method of consuming more than hearing from individuals who apply this understanding and live it each day in their personal lives. Thousands of individuals lost dramatic levels of weight without problems rather than regained it. One reader called Scott weighed an astounding 500 pounds. Scott couldn't tie his very own sneakers. His breathing was laboured, and he could walk only nine actions at a time. He was thirty-eight years aged. A doctor informed him that if he didn't undergo belly reduction surgery, he'd probably die within half a year. Scott spurned his doctor's guidance and instead made a decision to switch how he considered food and his method of eating by pursuing my high-nutrient meal strategy, which offered him with the nutrients, protein, and vitamin supplements he had a need to achieve good wellness. Because he right now eats for health, he can eat just as much as he wants, ignoring the scale fully. Today, Scott weighs 180 pounds and wants to exercise-a big differ from when he could not walk.

My individuals routinely lose up to 20 pounds through the first six weeks of changing their diet plan. And that's simply the start. More importantly, they typically get over diseases such as for example allergies, asthma, acne, headaches, high blood circulation pressure, diabetes, reflux esophagitis, lupus, kidney insufficiency, psoriasis, angina, cardiomyopathy, and multiple sclerosis-and they steadily get to get rid of their dependence on prescription drugs.

Though I have very long studied and utilized high- nutrient eating as a medical prescription for days gone by twenty-five years, actually I must admit to being amazed by a few of the phenomenal recoveries folks have reported if you ask me. Once, somebody asked whether this micronutrient-rich approach could change their hair back again to brownish from grey. "Of program not really," I answered. But, affirmed, on my website discussion board, two different people commented that it experienced occurred to them. I couldn't believe it. Similarly, among my sufferers had hepatitis C prior to starting my eating design. I didn't believe this high-nutrient eating design would remedy his hepatitis contamination and liver injury; nevertheless, after some right time, his hepatitis C disappeared. I had to do it again the blood tests 3 x to believe it. Seeing such dramatic recoveries from what exactly is conventionally considered irreversible illnesses excited me, making me even more adamant that delicious method of eating can result in medical transformations for an incredible number of Americans.

The total results and success stories are astounding. They come from folks of different back again- grounds, from different age groups, and they all began their journeys for different factors. Yet what they talk about in common is all of them are now in excellent wellness. For most of the Intuitive eating's achievement; however, I quickly found realize that science-based details about nutrition only wasn't enough. With these details available to such a wide audience, why would a lot of people neglect to recognize there have to protect their valuable health insurance and lose weight? Why would they become unable and unready to change? Why would they like to reject unassailable, scientific, and significantly effective advice? I'll let you know why, due to the mind-boggling twin powers of meals preference and meals addiction.

Just like the classic victim, we actually grow to love things that kill us-in this case, unhealthy food. Unhealthy eating styles and meals addictions have both used control of our brains, and this dependence on certain foods is frequently as deadly as many other addictions.

The standard American diet plan (SAD) is eliminating us. Rather than providing us with these basic needs once and for all health, it has created a country where disease and persistent illness are believed to be unavoidable and just another organic consequence of ageing. Carrying excess fat is the primary reason behind type 2 diabetes; it accelerates atherosclerosis and death from cardiovascular disease. In just a matter of years, excess body weight is usually projected to overtake smoking as the root cause of loss of life in the USA. By enough time, most Americans reach age fifty, they are already addicted to prescription drugs, and almost fifty per cent of People in America still die of heart attacks and strokes. You don't need to be one of them. Twenty-eight million Americans have problems with the crippling discomfort of osteoarthritis. You do not have to be one of these. Thirty-five million Americans have problems with persistent headaches. You don't need to be one of them. You simply don't need to be sick.

Today, 475 million adults all over the world suffer from obesity. That's a 50 per cent increase since 1980. Simultaneously, the amount of over- excess weight adults is fast approaching 1 billion, plus some 200 million school-age kids are already overweight, which means almost 1. 7 billion individuals are either overweight or obese. One nearly 7 billion people!

In the USA alone, about two-thirds of People in America are overweight, based on the National Institutes of Wellness (NIH). But this doesn't tell the complete story. Both NIH and the Globe Health Business define an "obese" person to possess a body mass index (BMI) of 25. This implies that a woman who is 5 feet 5 inches tall is considered a standard pounds at 150 pounds, and a guy whose 5 feet 10 inches tall is considered regular at 175 pounds. This man and female may carry between 20 and 30 pounds of disease- leading to excess fat around their waists. However, they would be considered healthy and match by today's standards. This is not accurate to look at a person with that very much fat normal or healthy. If you look at societies or groups of individuals who live longer than average, you'll discover average group BMIs between 18 and 22-nowhere close to the American regular of 25. For instance, the Okinawa Centenarian Study-which examined a lot more than 1000 centenarians from Okinawa, Japan, over twenty-five years from the mid-1970s to 2001-found that the common BMI of the studied adults was 20.4; The Adventist Health Study-who follow a mainly vegan diet-found an identical result. This twelve-year prospective study of thirty-four thousand middle-aged and elderly Adventists without preexisting illnesses, no background of smoking, cardiovascular system disease, malignancy, or stroke exposed a primary positive relation between a lesser BMI and longevity. An Adventist with a BMI greater than 23 does experience a higher threat of premature death.

Just what exactly can we study from these studies? Based on the data, the utmost acceptable weight generates a BMI of around 22.5, not 25. This implies that the recommended healthful weight for a 5-foot-10-inches adult male is usually between 130 and 160 pounds, and for 5-foot-5-inches adult female is 108 to 135 pounds. That is a large difference from the suitable (not obese) American BMI of 25, which allows 150 pounds for a female and 175 pounds for a guy. Based on the Okinawan and Adventist regular BMI, about 85 per cent of Americans are overweight, not really the 66 per cent based on the NIH. The common American is definitely heavier and sicker than she or he even realizes. All due to the typical American diet. Hardly anyone can get away its destructive effects. Why else would 90 per cent of everybody older than sixty-five be taking medicines to lessen his or her blood circulation pressure and/or cholesterol? The end result is this: In the event that you eat American meals, you will inevitably develop the illnesses common in America, you shall become overweight, and you will ultimately develop high blood circulation pressure and raised cholesterol (the signs of bloodstream vessel and cardiovascular disease), just like everyone else.

We now contemplate it normal to reduce youthful vigour inside our thirties, carry a supplementary 30 to 40 pounds, live with chronic illness inside our past due forties and fifties, and endure our final years completely reliant on others. But this is simply not normal. This is actually the consequence of a lifelong design of harmful living and misguided info. Instead of dreading deterioration and an increasing number of ailments and medications as we approach later years, we should anticipate enjoying an active existence well into our nineties. This might seem like an outrageous expectation because the majority of us spend eternity eating an unhealthy diet. Today even, too many folks continue to skip the connection between what we consume and how we experience emotionally and actually. Nor can we find out why it appears so difficult to remain at our youthful adult weight.

But it's not as well late.

A high-nutrient diet will certainly reduce your desire to have high-calorie, low-nutrient foods. Within weeks, your taste buds will change, and you'll weary in the processed foods you once believed you could by no means live without. You'll experience more satisfied consuming fewer calorie consumption than you were consuming before. The result is lasting health and long term weight loss. So a lot of my visitors have dropped 100 pounds or even more following my suggestions; they have dropped that much within twelve months, and they have held that weight off for a long time.

THE FINISH of Dieting goes a step beyond Intuitive eating. Not merely does it solution why eating health- completely often appears so difficult, it empowers you with the desire and capability to do so. In the next pages, I talk about the technology and the solutions behind how exactly to rid yourself once and for all of the meals addictions sabotaging your wellbeing. I construct an easy-to-follow eating system you start with a fourteen-day group of easy-to-make, delicious meals that will steadily transform your food preferences, while concurrently recalibrating your palate. I guide your meal options through the first section of the program, so you don't need to think or be concerned in what you're eating-you can merely eat tasty dishes manufactured from fantastic health- assisting foods. In the next area of the programme, I flood the body with nutrition to heal and detoxify it, using very foods in an effort to promote wellness and longevity. By completing and sticking with the program, your BMI shall fall below 22.5 and stay there for the others you will ever have.

A diet can just be looked at successful if the meals you eat helps longevity and protect you against cardiovascular disease, stroke, dementia, and malignancy. This nutritarian diet design is the just dietary and nutritional system that guarantees dramatic excess weight reduction without calorie counting. Additionally, it is the just dietary and nutritional plan that explains how to drive back disease while simultaneously significantly increasing your lifespan. Your threat of a coronary attack and/or stroke will almost disappear, and your threat of tumour can plummet by a lot more than 90 per cent, while your daily life expectancy can boost by two decades. Incredible statements, yes, but that is a reality with substantial scientific support. I've observed such outcomes for a lot more than twenty-five years. Forget calorie consumption. The trick of living well is about micronutrients. Eating healthfully and consuming the proper assortment and quantity of nutrients outcomes in consistent, long-term health benefits. Getting healthful and maintaining well balanced, healthful weights are achieved just by concentrating on the dietary quality of your meal. Contrary to standard thinking, it isn't just how much you take in that determines your body weight; it's everything you eat.

Nutritional quality determines your mental, physical, and psychological health-from brain function and an elevated disease fighting capability to happiness and physical well-being. The primary criterion you should think about when choosing what things to eat is which foods are most favourable to your long-term survival. A diet plan style incorporating longevity- advertising foods enables you to try out all sorts of delicious quality recipes, which allows you to continue this new method of eating through the entire rest you will ever have. Any diet you adopt temporarily only results in short-term benefits because eventually your body and your weight change back to the diet you will remain in the long term. I want to repeat that again: Whatever you adopt temporarily just begets temporary outcomes, and fluctuating your body weight up and down isn't life- span favourable. People often view diet programs as a belief program, picking the one which is most closely aligned with their dietary philosophy or food preferences. They often criticize any system that conflicts with these choices. Real science, however, does not have any philosophy or predetermined agenda; it simply flows inexorably from the preponderance of the data. Are you a scientific thinker? Do you want to view reality and allow chips to fall with the data? Remember: Food choices are learned and may be changed.

We have cared for a lot more than 10 thousand people, the majority of whom set foot in my own office unhappy, sick, and overweight. That they had tried each and every dietary craze without achievement. After following my plan, they found out the superior health they always wanted and dropped the weight they always dreamed of losing. Even better, it was kept by them off. For the very first time in their lives, that they had a feeding on the style that didn't keep them starving or unsatisfied. Most of all, they were in a position to stop acquiring their medicines, which had become unneeded.

In the last three decades, I've reviewed a lot more than twenty thousand scientific tests on human nutrition. For this reason, I can state with certainty that is usually the place and today is the period to begin your wellbeing revival. I've seen the results of this plan doing his thing on a large number of people with a wide variety of diseases and health issues, from migraines and allergies to cardiovascular disease and diabetes. The end result is, it functions. Nutritional excellence may be the most effective way to discover long term healthy weight reduction, prevent and invert disease, and end a few of today's most chronic degenerative illnesses.

Your body is a self-therapeutic machine when you supply it with an optimal nutritional environment, and the information presented in this book is the quickest and most effective way to create that environment. In case you have high blood circulation pressure, high cholesterol, diabetes, cardiovascular disease, indigestion, headaches, asthma, exhaustion, body aches, or discomfort- or if you would like to avoid yourself from developing these chronic conditions- this may be the arrange for you. This fresh diet style can allow you in order to avoid angioplasty, bypass medical procedures, and other invasive methods. In the event that you aren't however ill, it could make sure you do not have heart episodes, strokes, or dementia in your old age. It can reduce and eventually get rid of your need for prescription drugs. In short, it can allow you to optimize your health and potentially save your life. And it could do all this while raising the enjoyment you get from meals.

A lot of you have this publication because you would like to lose weight. I wish to assure you that you'll lose all of the weight that you would like, even if diet programs have failed you previously. This is usually the most reliable weight-loss plan ever, and the email address details are permanent, not temporary. Equally essential may be the protection from severe diseases in your own future that this plan gives. The most efficient healthcare is self-care. Medicines and doctors can't grant you superb health insurance and protect you from disease and suffering. Almost every doctor does know this. The dietary excellence I explain in the following can prevent and actually reverse most medical complications within three to half a year. That is a bold state, but the facts-supported by scientific research-display that lots of the tragedies we encounter in today's world are the consequence of nutritional folly. While weight reduction is important, it isn't our main objective. It is an enjoyable and regular by-product on the path to the principal goal: great health. First-class health is definitely marked by an exceedingly long and fairly disease-free lifespan, and countless research reveals that individuals with superior wellness are thin. By teaching you how exactly to achieve superior health, your ideal weight will normally follow. You will understand the physical cravings that trigger overeating, along with the psychological factors that will help you switch this pattern of usage. Applying the info in this reserve to your life can help you create new, healthy behaviours that may eventually become effortless. You will finally maintain control of your health destiny.

This plan will not include counting calories, measuring food portion sizes, or weighing. It doesn't depend on gimmicks or fads. You can end searching for that magic answer since there is no magic remedy. No reddish berry ketones. No green coffees. No purple tulip nectar or dark salt from the white cliffs of Dover. Actually, we almost always, later on, discover that the merchandise that gave us wish was simply hype and that searching for a magic pill causes harm. Whenever a supplement or medicine doesn't meet up with your nutritive requirements, it really is typically toxic and may enhance the damage the effect of a toxic diet.

As we struggled with these issues, we started to explore a few of the popular literature that suggested a 180-level departure from dieting. It proposed a means of consuming that allowed for just about any and all meals choices, regardless of nutrition. Our preliminary reactions were extremely sceptical, if not down- correct rejecting. We reacted with self-righteous indignation. How could we, as nutritionists (authorized dietitians), trained to consider the connections between nourishment and health, sanction a means of eating that appeared to reject the foundation of our understanding and philosophy?

The struggle continued. Healthy eating plans did not help people maintain long-term weight control; the "nutritional waste strategy" was a dangerous choice. The suggestion to ignore nutrition and disregard the way the body seems in response to eating "whatever you want" discount rates the respect for one's body that comes combined with the gift of life. Finally, we resolved the conflict by developing the process of intuitive consumption. This book may be a bridge between its growing movement against diet and the medical community. While the anti-diet movement avoids dieting and blames body acceptance (thankfully), it often doesn't address health risks. How can you reconcile the problems of forbidden foods but still eat healthy, without dieting? We will let you know how in this post.

In case you are like most of our customers, you are tired of dieting but at the same time terrified of eating. Most of our customers feel uncomfortable within their bodies, but don't understand how to change. Intuitive eating provides a new way of eating that is ultimately hassling free and healthy for the brain and body. It really is an activity that frees the chains of the diet (which can only cause deprivation, rebellion and weight gain in extension). This means getting back again to your roots-trusting the body and its signals.

Intuitive eating cannot only change the relationship with food; it can change your daily life.

Intuitive Feeding on includes the principles of mindful eating; in addition, it has a broader philosophy, addressing the problems of cognitive distortions and psychological eating. It includes seeing realization as a central point in consumption, physical activity/movement in relation to feeling good, rejecting the mentality of the diet, using nutritional information without judging and respecting the body, regardless of how you feel about your shape. Intuitive nutrition is undoubtedly a dynamic procedure that integrates the tuning of the brain, body and meals. For those with feeding problems, conscious and intuitive feeding can help facilitate normal feeding.

CHAPTER 4:

Arousing the Intuitive Eater: Stages

The journey to Intuitive Eating is like going for a cross-district climbing trip. Before you really tie without anyone else climbing boots, you'd have to recognize what's in store all through your outing. While a road map is viable, it doesn't disclose what you'll be enough prepared, such as trail conditions, atmosphere, special touring detects, the kind of garments to put on, etc. The goal of this part is, for the most part, to help you comprehend what to envision all through your outing to Intuitive Eating.

Regardless of whether it's strolling or relearning an unmistakably all the more fulfilling eating plan, you will continue through numerous phases in transit. The amount of time that you should remain static in a specific stage is certainly a factor and amazingly individualized. For example, crossing new climbing trails relies on how physically fit you are, the way you adapt to worry with a new path, exactly how much time you have to climb, and the choice of climbing trails. In like manner, your adventure back again to Intuitive Eating relies on how protracted you've been dieting, how emphatically settled in your everyday diet believing is the means by which long you've been utilizing suppers to deal with life, that you are so arranged to confide in yourself, and that you are so prepared to put weight decrease on the storage compartment burner and see how to turn into an Intuitive Eater the essential objective.

Now and again, you'll move in reverse and advances among the stages. In the event that you recognize that is an ordinary segment of the procedure, it can assist you with continuing without inclination that you will fall away from the faith or not so much gaining ground. Think about this circumstance: You are on a mobile path and experience a fork in the road that is difficult to unravel together with your path map. Do you go legitimately to one side or left? You consider for quite a while and pick to go remaining. While strolling, you place something you've in no way, shape or form seen previously, a sparkling green caterpillar shimmying up a purple bloom. A couple of activities ahead, you find a novel fowl. In any case, a couple of strategies past these wonders of character are a huge rock flagging that you locate an inappropriate course. You pivot, return to the fork, and think about the other course. Was this temporary re-routing an exercise in futility?

No! So also, in connection to Intuitive Eating, you will require numerous turns and test out new contemplations and practices. You may locate that subsequent to creating recognizable advancement, and you return to old procedures are terrible and unfulfilling. In any case, such as gaining "an inappropriate" course on the grand trekking trail, you'll see that outings into matured expending examples can be used as learning encounters. (Numerous climbers wouldn't ordinarily scold themselves to be uncertain of what direction to take; rather, they'd be grateful for the disclosures of character that a blocked course offered.) It's imperative that you help yourself out and welcome the preparation that turns out from experience. This procedure includes originating from a position of interest rather than a position of judgment, along these lines whatever you do; don't crush yourself up intellectually!

Intuitive Eating is very not equivalent to dieting. Dieters, for the most part, get disappointed on the off chance that they don't follow the dietary plan way decisively as endorsed. We've seen numerous a relentless dieters simply have an off -base change at one feast, be critical for that error, and "blow" the dietary plan for that day time or end of the week or in reality longer! Recall that the outing to Intuitive Eating is typically a procedure, loaded up with good and bad times, un-like dieting where in actuality the regular desire is unquestionably direct advancement (losing a specific measure of abundance weight in a specific time span).

The road to Intuitive Eating is like obtaining a long haul common store. Over the long haul, you will see an arrival on speculation, paying little mind to the everyday vacillations of the money markets. It is customary and anticipated. How amusing that individuals have been prepared that, in financial matters, the everyday changes in the cash markets are typical, and once in a while is there a moment get-rich fix, yet, in the multibillion-dollar, a year pounds misfortune business, "get slender quick" might be the main target for accomplishment. We are contributed, rather, in helping you give harmony to your expending presence and self-perception. In connection to this objective, remember Webster's portrayal of procedure: "a continuous advancement including numerous alterations" and "a particular way to deal with accomplishing something, including various advances or activities by and large."

Much like any procedure, it's essential that you remain centred in, and develop from the numerous experiences you will experience. Assuming, in any case, you focus on the result (which for some, people is fat or the number of pounds lost), it could make you experience overpowered and debilitated, and wrap up disrupting the strategy. Rather, if your air conditioning information little changes in transit and worth the preparation encounters (that may in some cases be disappointing), it can assist you with adhering to the Intuitive Eating course and push ahead. When you truly become an Intuitive Eater, you will consistently check out your inward insight, and you may feel better on a basic level, body, and soul.

Now, we feel it is important to explain the issue of the mission for weight reduction. For a few, the body will return to its normal abundance weight level, which might be not exactly your present pounds and remain there. To watch if this relates to you, ask yourself the following inquiries:

Perhaps you have routinely destroyed from agreeable totality level? Perform you routinely gorge when you're getting arranged for the following diet (understanding that there will turn into a ton of foods you won't be allowed to eat on the dietary plan)? Perform your gorge as an adapting framework in troublesome events or to fill period when you're exhausted? Maybe you have been impervious to work out?

Do you only exercise in the event that you are dieting? Do you skip foods or hold back to eat until you're insatiably hungry, possibly to find that you indulge when you at long last expend? Do you are feeling remorseful; either when you indulge or when you take in all that you call a "poor food," which results in all the more overeating? If you addressed "yes" for a few of the vast majority of these inquiries, after that all things considered, your present weight might be more prominent than the weight the body is intended to keep up. Furthermore, it is likely you will have the option to return to your common, sound weight, because of this procedure. Be that as it may, recall, weight decrease should be put on the storage compartment burner. In the event that you focus on weight reduction, it'll meddle with your ability to settle on decisions predicated on your intuitive signs.

When you've surrendered the pointlessness of dieting perpetually, you'll wind up eating far fewer suppers with a craving to see customary movement in your day by day life. You'll find that the body feels so far superior when your midsection isn't stuffed, at whatever point your muscle tissue is conditioned, just as your heart is coordinate. You will likewise find that as your contemplations about your eating and body begin to transform, you will encounter an all the more loosening up feeling, rather than the incessant foundation stress that weaving machines each supper decision. Nonetheless, if you keep on focusing on weight decrease as the objective, you'll get tangled up in the matured diet-attitude figuring, which won't serve you.

Throughout the years, we've seen our people continue through a five-organize movement in figuring out how to be an Intuitive Eater. The following segment can assist you with getting an idea of what things to expect inside your very own adventure.

Stage One: Readiness-Hitting Diet Plan Bottom

This is the place numerous individuals start. You are agonizingly conscious that each attempt to get in shape is made in "falling flat." You are wary of esteeming every day predicated on whether the level is as a rule up or down a pound or two (or on the off chance that you indulged your prior day). You envision and stress over dinners constantly. You talk the prohibitive food visit "Just in the event that I didn't have to watch my overabundance weight, I could expend that," or "I encountered two treats I truly was awful today."

As of now, your weight might be higher than any time in recent memory, or, without significantly over-weight, you lose and increase five or ten pounds to such an extent and rapidly as you wash your garments in addition to they get filthy again! You have lost contact with organic food longings and satiety signals. You have overlooked all that you truly prefer to expend and rather eat all that you figure you "should" eat. Your association with dinners has built up a poor tone, and you fear to eat the foods you like since you're apprehensive it'll be difficult to stop. At the point when you yield to the enticement of illegal foods, it's normal to indulge them, since you are feeling remorseful. However, you earnestly pledge you won't ever eat them again.

It's not bizarre to get that you take into comfort, occupy, or even numb yourself from your very own emotions. On the off chance that that is the situation, you will feel that an incredible evaluation offers been blurred by obsession thinking about suppers and by careless expending. The self-perception is negative-you don't simply like the manner in which you show up and feel inside your body, and confidence is reduced. You have found from your experience that dieting won't work-you have arrived in a desperate predicament and experience stuck, debilitated, and disheartened.

This stage proceeds until you select that you will be troubled eating and living along these lines you will be prepared to accomplish something positive about it. Your first contemplations may veer toward finding another diet to determine your issues. Yet, very quickly, you comprehend that you can't do that one until kingdom come. On the off chance that that is the place you find yourself, you at that point are set up for the method that will empower you to get back again to eating intuitively.

Stage Two: Exploration-Conscious Learning And Quest For Pleasure

That is a phase of investigation and disclosure. You will continue through a phase of hyper consciousness to incredibly help reacquaint yourself together with your intuitive signs: hunger, season inclinations, and satiety.

This stage resembles figuring out how precisely to drive a vehicle. For the beginner driver, simply getting the vehicle out from the garage requires a lot of conscious deduction, loaded up with a psychological agenda: Place the principle component in the start, make certain the contraption is in diversion zone or impartial, start the motor, check the rearview reflect, remove the hand brake, and so forth. This hyper consciousness is basic to secure every one of the means required simply to acquire that vehicle into Drive! In a similar inclination, you will focus in on subtleties of eating which have advanced without such centred reasoning. (In any case, this is basic to recover the Intuitive Eater in you.)

It might seem clumsy and awkward, fanatical even. In any case, hyper consciousness varies than over the top considering. Over the top reasoning is generally unavoidable and is viewed as stress. It fills your brain during most of the day and prevents you from considering much else. Hyperconsciousness is increasingly specific. It zooms in the event that you have thought about food, yet leaves totally when the eating experience is finished. What's more, like the means required stresses become autopilot for the accomplished driver, Intuitive Eating will eventually get experienced without this fundamental ungainliness.

You may accept that you are in a hyperconscious state more often than not during this stage. This may feel awkward at first just as maybe even abnormal. Keep in mind, a ton of your prior eating was either primarily thoughtless or diet plan coordinated.

In this stage, you'll begin to make harmony with food giving yourself unqualified consent to expend. This part may feel frightening, and you may choose to move gradually (inside your solace level). Become acquainted with to wipe out blame incited eating and begin to find the requirement for the fulfilment component with food. The significantly progressively cheerful you are while expending, the substantially less you see food on the off chance that you are not hungry you won't wind up being lurking here and there. You will explore different avenues regarding foods that you probably won't have eaten for quite a while. This comprises of sifting through your exact food needs and needs. You may even find that you don't simply like the kind of a couple of the foods you've been longing for! (Remember those long stretches of dieting, or eating all that you "should" simply serve to disengage you from your own inner eating travel and genuine food decisions.) Become acquainted with to respect your food yearnings and perceive the body markers that show the innumerable degrees of appetite. Become acquainted with, to separate these organic pointers from the enthusiastic markers that may likewise trigger eating.

In this stage, you may find that you will eat bigger degrees of foods than the body needs. It will be difficult to regard your totality as of now since you will require time to try out the amount it requires to satisfy a denied sense of taste. What's more, it requires some serious energy that you ought to create trust with suppers again and comprehend that it's really okay to expend. By what means will you respect completion, on the off chance that you are not absolutely sure it's okay to eat the specific food, or if you fear it won't become there tomorrow?

In the event that you have recently been putting on overabundance weight, weight gain typically stops or is restricted to just a couple of pounds. At the point when you have been utilizing suppers inwardly, you may find that you will begin to feel your emotions and may encounter uneasiness, pity, or really sadness on occasion. Most of your eating could be foods that are heavier in fat and sugar than you've been familiar with in spite of the fact that you may have been eating huge degrees of these food types furtively or with blame. How you eat in this stage will never be the example that you'll set up or requirement for a lifetime. You will see that your nourishing soundness is for the most part helter-skelter and you probably won't feel physically alongside focuses during this time. That is all standard and anticipated. You have to let yourself continue through this phase for such a long time as you need. Keep in mind, and you are creating for quite a while of hardship, troublesome self-talk, and blame. You are re-building positive food experiences, much the same as a strand of pearls. Every feast experience, similar to each pearl, may seem immaterial, however, by and large, they change lives.

Stage Three: Crystallization

In this stage, you will experience the primary renewals of the Intuitive Eating style which has consistently been a piece of you, yet was covered underneath the flotsam and jetsam of dieting. At the point when you enter this stage, a great deal of the investigation work from the earlier stage begins to solidify and feels as if strong conducts change. Your thoughts regarding food are not any more over the top. You barely need to stay aware of the hyperconsciousness about eating that was initially required. Thusly, your eating choices don't require very as particularly coordinated accepted. Rather, you find that your food choices and reactions to natural pointers are principally intuitive.

You have a bigger feeling of trust-both in your to pick what you really need to eat and in the undeniable reality that your natural signs are depend-capable. You are advantageous with your food choices and will start to see expanded satisfaction at your suppers.

Now, you respect your appetite most of the time and it's less difficult to perceive what you feel simply like eating in the event that you are hungry. You keep on creating harmony with food.

What feels new in this stage is that it's more straightforward to require some investment out in the midst of your food to intentionally check exactly how a lot of your paunch is topping off. It is conceivable to watch your completion and regard the presence of that sign, regardless of whether you find that you as often as possible eat past the totality tag. Precisely like when a toxophilite requires focus on a crisp objective, it frequently requires catching numerous bolts before figuring out how precisely to come to the bull's-eye. You may at present be picking recently prohibited foods most of the time, yet you will find that you don't require as a lot of them to satisfy you.

On the off chance that you've been a genuinely signaled eater, you'll become very skilled at isolating natural yearning markers from passionate appetite. Because of this lucidity, more than not frequently, you'll be encountering your feelings and discovering techniques to com-stronghold and occupy yourself without the use of food.

Be certain you put weight decrease on the storage compartment burner. Much more significant than abundance weight reduction, is the inclination of well-turning out to be and strengthening that become-gins to happen. You won't any longer feel vulnerable and miserable. You will begin to regard your body and get that in case you're over your regular weight, it's because of the dieting attitude, rather than absence of resolve.

Stage 4: The Intuitive Eater Awakens

By enough time you arrive at this stage, all the work you have just been doing comes full circle in an agreeable, free-streaming eating style. You consistently pick what you truly need to eat when you are ravenous. Since you comprehend that you can have altogether more suppers, based on your personal preference, when you are starving, it's anything but difficult to stop eating when you are feeling serenely full. You may begin to find that you pick more advantageous foods, not on the grounds that you envision you should, but since you are feeling better physically when you take along these lines. The pressing need to demonstrate to yourself that you could have recently prohibited foods could have reduced. You truly know and trust these foods will be there, and on the off chance that you need to eat them truly, you can-in this manner they drop their charming quality. Chocolate starts to shield myself against a similar mental implication as a peach. You won't any more drawn out need to test yourself, just as your hardship reaction with suppers will be no more. At the point when you do choose the foods you used to limit, you'll get extraordinary delight, and feel content with a particularly littler amount than beforehand, and without blame. (At the point when you are feeling regretful eating a suppers, it removes a great deal of the happiness from eating.) In the event that managing your emotions have been hard for you, you'll be less reluctant to see them, and be increasingly capable at plunking down with them. Finding refreshing choices to occupy and comfort yourself when required can be normal for you.

Your food talk and self talk will be certain and non-basic. Your tranquility settlement with suppers is solidly settled, and you will have discharged any contention or remaining blame about dinner's decisions you have hauled around.

You have quit being furious together with your body and making ill bred input about it. You regard it and acknowledge there are a wide range of shapes and sizes on the planet. At this genuine point, and if it's intended to be, the body will be coming to moving toward its natural weight.

Stage Five: The Ultimate Stage-Treasure The Pleasure

Right now your Intuitive Eater has been guaranteed. You will confide in your body's intuitive capacities it will be easy to respect your yearning and regard totality. At long last, you will encounter no blame about your feast decisions or amounts. Since you like your sentimental relationship to dinners and fortune the fulfillment that eating currently offers you, you will dispose of unacceptable eating conditions and unappealing foods.

You should encounter benefiting from in the most ideal of conditions as opposed to corrupt it with enthusiastic misery. You will encounter an internal conviction to quit utilizing food to deal with enthusiastic circumstances, if that is your propensity. At the point when sentiments become too astounding, you will see that you'll much rather adapt to your feelings or occupy yourself at times from their site with anything separated from food.

Since your eating style has become a wellspring of joy rather than a suffering, you will encounter sustenance and development in various manners.

The duty of activity will be evacuated, and practicing will begin to look luring to you. Exercise won't be used as a driving strain to catch fire more calories; rather, you feel com-mitted to exercise with an end goal to feel much improved, and intellectually physically. In like manner, food won't be another instrument to make you feel terrible about how you eat; rather, it transforms into an approach to feeling as in reality great and solid as could be expected under the circumstances.

At the point when you arrive at a definitive stage, your bodyweight will sink into what's normal for you-a spot that is agreeable and befitting your height and body outline. In the event that your bodyweight was at that point ordinary, you will find that you'll keep up it without exertion and you will be freed of the mental good and bad times that go with the confinement/overeating cycles.

Finally, you will encounter enabled and shielded from outside powers telling you what and exactly the amount to eat, and how the body should look. You will feel clear of the duty of dieting. What's more, you'll be an Intuitive Eater again.

That you can do it!

These stages and the progressions that happen with your eating and considerations may seem outlandish. Or on the other hand, it may show up excessively startling. For instance, the very idea of giving yourself unrestricted authorization to eat may seem unnerving and you may expect that you'll never stop eating or putting on abundance weight. The remainder of the distribution clarifies in extraordinary fine detail how precisely to execute every rule, why it truly is required, and the explanation behind it. Also, you will figure out how extra interminable dieters became Intuitive Eaters and how it changed their lives. By enough time you wrap up this book, you will unquestionably realize that you also may turn into an Intuitive Eater, and forestall the franticness of dieting.

CHAPTER 5:

Guideline One: Reject the diet Mentality

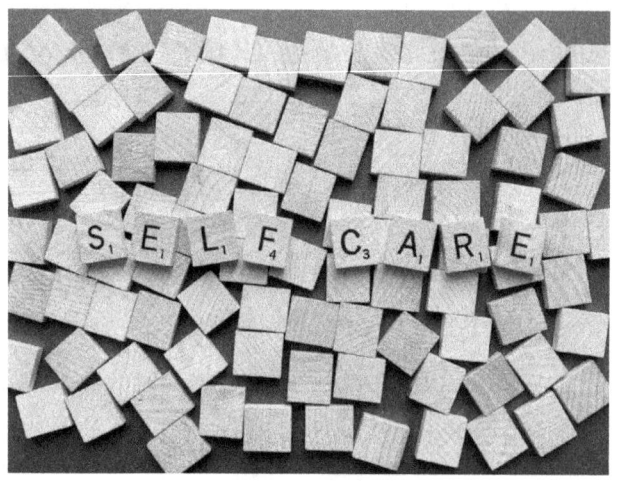

E liminate diet books and magazine articles that give you false weight loss expectations quickly, effectively and forever. Get irate at the untruths which have driven you to feel like you were bombing each time a crisp diet plan quit working and you got back all the weight. If you permit really one little want to wait that a crisp and better diet might be prowling close by, it'll keep you from turning out to be clear to rediscover Intuitive Eating. In case you're similar to most of clients we see, the idea of not dieting could be startling (despite the fact that you comprehend that you can't force down one more diet program or drink). It's customary to encounter panicky about letting continue of dieting, especially when the globe around you is for the most part on some diet. It's been the main gadget you have perceived to lose pounds (yet incidentally). Winding up in a real predicament level is an incapacitating sense-doomed if you diet and accursed if you don't. A significant number of our clients feel caught between two clashing apprehensions: "Effectively keep dieting, I'll ruin my digestion and put on weight" and "Effectively quit dieting I'll put on increasingly overabundance weight." Other basic feelings of fear that individuals hear are:

FEAR: Easily quit dieting, I won't quit eating.

REALITY: Dieting is generally the outcome in for overeating. Of program it's difficult to abstain from eating when you've been under expending and confining dinners. It's a standard reaction to starvation (you'll discover increasingly about that inside the following section). However, when the body learns (and believes) that you'll not starve it anymore (through dieting), the outrageous drive for eating will diminish.

FEAR: I don't see how to eat when I'm not dieting.

REALITY: When you exile diet programs and be an Intuitive Eater, you'll be benefiting from because of inside signs, which may control your eating. That resembles figuring out how precisely to swim for the absolute first time. The sense to be encompassed by water could be frightening to the beginner swimmer, when completely submerged particularly. In like manner, being encompassed by dinners could be alarming to the ceaseless dieter, who's figuring out how precisely to eat once more. In any case, you'll not make sense of how to swim by just remaining at the upside of the pool (while accepting that figuring out how precisely to swim is an incredible thing). First you start by considering going all in and figuring out how to take in the water. In the end you will put your brain in the water in the event that you are prepared and you get helpful.

FEAR: I am out of control.

REALITY: Control is definitely not a worry in Intuitive Eating. Or maybe, you will rely on your inner signs, rather than on outside components and authority numbers (whom will undoubtedly challenge). No one might be the expert of "you." Just you know your thoughts, sentiments, and encounters. Become acquainted with to confide in your inward astuteness and can figure out how to focus on and respect your inside prompts (both physical and mental), which feels engaging.

THE DIET VOID

For some, a person dieting is an approach to deal with life, from topping off period, to filling in as representative of authority over your day by day life. Think about the changing occasions throughout your life where you began a diet plan. How as often as possible did your diet programs concur with troublesome events or changes in your everyday life? It's normal to begin a diet through the accompanying presence changes: moving from youth to youthfulness, going out, wedding, beginning a new activity, or while experiencing conjugal troubles. While dieting may have been worthless, it offered pleasure and expectation the elation of quick weight reduction and the invigoration of watching the level inch descending. The desire that this diet plan will work out; It's like prone to a hairdresser for a new trim, with the desire that it'll upset how you show up and feel about yourself and maybe completely changes you.

Anyway when you state farewell to the fervor and joy of dieting, you'll likewise become letting continue of the bogus wish and dissatisfactions from dieting. There's a social segment to dieting that you may miss, diet plan holding. At the point when you decide to stop dieting, you might be astonished how often new diet plans and dieting will be the subjects of discourse at parties, with dear companions, at work-and right now you won't wind up being playing that game. It may feel simply like an absolute necessity see film numerous individuals are discussing, just you haven't saw it and furthermore have no plans to see it either. You may feel somewhat ignored, confined. Keep in mind, inasmuch as by and by there is money to be created; there will be a new contrivance or diet plan for a moment weight reduction fix. At one phase, the maker of something known as "Sleepers Dieter" asserted to incredibly assist individuals with achieving higher weight reduction during rest. Visit about dreaming! The producer was fined by the FTC to make unverified cases. Be that as it may, individuals still dished out the measure of cash on account of this new trick.

The One-Last-Diet Trap

Stage one to turning into an Intuitive Eater is to dismiss the dietary plan attitude. However despite the fact that you come to conditions with the vanity and harm that dieting releases on your body (and brain), it's somewhat a troublesome initially rung on the stepping stool. To get yourself out from the last-chance diet plan trap, you need to come to conditions with the established truth that dieting doesn't work and can, really, be unsafe. (Remember, an assortment of study shows that the make a move of dieting raises your risk of putting on much more weight. This is valid for children, young people, and grown-ups. We imagine that if individuals really realized that starting a better eating routine could make the body put on increasingly abundance weight, they would not so much decline the vain dieting course.) Maybe you're slanted to contend, be that as it may, that you'll encounter better about yourself when you lose the abundance weight. Yet, thinks about have shown that enhancements in mental prosperity associated with weight reduction are basically as present moment as the pounds dropped and recovered. The "extraordinary feelings" decrease with recaptured pounds, and existing issues of self-well worth and general passionate capacity return to introductory sums when the overabundance weight is recovered.

Pseudo-Dieting

Many customers state, "I've deserted dieting" anyway despite everything they have issues shaking the dietary plan mindset. They may be physically from a diet, anyway the dieting contemplations remain. The issue is normally that dieting contemplations for the most part bring about diet-like practices, which transforms into pseudo-dieting or oblivious dieting. Therefore, these clients will even now endure the average reactions of dieting, yet it's especially harder to distinguish (and they truly feel wild with their eating). Pseudo-dieting practices aren't normally clear to the individual occupied with them. Recollect that eating is surely basic that it's difficult to get objective. It could be hard to procure the escape clauses inside your own expending mindset/conduct if you don't know very well what you are scanning for. To the stun of our clients they customarily don't find that they have just been pseudo-dieting until on the whole we assess their Intuitive Eating diary. Here are a couple of instances of pseudo-dieting:

a. Meticulously checking starch grams might be the cutting edge version of tallying calories. While monitoring what you eat offers its merits, the demonstration of tallying sugar grams to control weight is quite not quite the same as checking calories. Many ceaseless dieters are benefits at apportioning their sugar grams for the afternoon and they are caught.

b. Eating just "free from any potential harm" foods. This outcome in staying with sans fat of charge as well as low-calorie foods, wind up being-yond tallying starch grams. For example, one customer wouldn't regularly eat any dinners that recorded a few gram of muscle to fat ratio on the supper's name, whatever her all out muscle versus fat and calorie utilization for your day was. Keep in mind, in any case, that one suppers, one feast, or 1 day won't represent the deciding moment your prosperity or your weight.

c. Eating just now and again of the day, regardless of whether you are hungry, is normally a typical extra propensity from dieting, particularly not eating following a specific time of night, such as after 6 P.M. Rude awakening: Our life structures don't punch period timekeepers; we don't all of a sudden mood killer our requirement for vitality at a particular time. This can particularly be viewed as an issue for a dieter who practices after work, returns late around 7:30 P.M., and chooses it's also late to expend for fear that the overabundance fat meter is certainly in high apparatus. In spite of the fact that it is sensible never to need to visit bed on a total stomach since it will be terrible, to deny a destitute body any dinners or vitality can be outlandish.

d. Paying compensation for eating "poor" foods such as treats, cheesecake, or frozen yogurt. The punishment run from avoiding another feast, eating less, vowing to become "extraordinary" tomorrow, or performing additional activity.

e. Reducing on food, especially when feeling fat or at whatever point an uncommon occasion like a wedding or course get-together comes up. While diminishing sounds guiltless a lot of, it's astounding how as often as possible this gets carried on in the kind of oblivious under eating. Keep in mind, under eating for the most part triggers overeating.

f. Pacifying food desires by drinking coffee or diet pop. That is a typical dieting procedure to mitigate food longings without eating or calorie utilization.

g. Limiting starches. We are struck by the measure of clients who proclaim they comprehend of the requirement for eating this sort of fuel, anyway eat an insufficient amount of starches, such as breads, pasta, rice, and so forth, since they're apprehensive they will put on weight.

h. Gaining a "bogus food experience" in open zones. You just eat what's "appropriate" before others. One client, Alice, ate a fantastic dinner with companions. At the point when the sweet plate landed around her really needed a touch of pie, yet battled the longing, since she wished to resemble the sound/weight-careful eater. For any case, on her benefit way home, the longing for the pie expand into a wild hankering. Alice ended at the shop, purchased a total pie, and ate one-fourth of it-much more than she'd have eaten experienced she respected her precise food inclination! This relational dieting conduct of increasing a bogus food experience exploded backward (and it much of the time does).

i. Competing with someone else who's dieting ... feeling committed to wind up being similarly high-minded (or significantly more). Since dieting can be viewed as an ethical characteristic inside our general public, it isn't bizarre that you'll get sucked into appearing temperate. This can just happen when companions, family, or a considerable other is dieting.

j. Second-speculating or judging all that you have the right to expend predicated on what you've eated promptly in the day, rather than on hunger signs. One client, Sally, ate two colossal dishes of puffed rice oat for breakfast subsequent to working for 60 minutes. She accepted that was an exorbitant measure of food and later on in the midmorning didn't enable herself to expend, in spite of the fact that she was voracious. Sally figured, "How may I be hungry only two hours when I had an enormous breakfast?" reality for Sally was that while her degree of food every morning was greater than her standard, it had been as yet deficient for the amount of activity she did. Her body was endeavoring to advise her, "I need more fuel." However Sally felt regretful to be ravenous. She additionally felt remorseful for eating an enormous breakfast, until she perceived that much of the time she had under eaten. Wish dinner or tidbit won't fit the "standard" part size from your very own dieting days; it by and large doesn't infer you are overeating!

k. Learning to be a veggie lover or expending a gluten gratis diet restricted to the reason for thinning down. A veggie lover way of life could be a sound method for expending and living, however on the off chance that it's grasped with a diet plan attitude; it turns out to be essentially another diet. For instance, Karen began eating meatless to lose overabundance weight. In any case, every month into her veggie lover eating, she began wanting meat. Nothing you've seen earlier had she encountered meats longings!

Karen saw she barely ever truly planned to transform into a veggie lover. She wasn't contemplating veggie lover eating for health or moral issues, similarly as a vehicle to get more fit, in this manner her diet back once more terminated.

The Dieter's Dilemma

Regardless of whether you are occupied with genuine dieting or pseudo-dieting, any sort of dieting will prompt confusions. The acquire vanity of dieting is typically depicted in the Dieter's Problem outline delivered by clinicians, John P. G and foreyt. Ken Goodrick, showed underneath. The Dieter's Problem is normally activated by the need to be slender, that prompts dieting. That is the point at which the issue unfurls. Dieting raises longings and desires for dinners. The dieter yield to the hankering, gorges, lastly recovers any lost overabundance weight. He's back again to where he started, with the underlying weight- or higher. When again the dieter persuades the need to be slim ... thusly another diet starts. The Dieter's Dilemma is certainly sustained and deteriorates with each difference in the everyday practice. The dieter can be heavier and feels much increasingly wild with eating.

Instructions To Reject The Dietary Plan Mentality

To disregard the dieting legend and the dieting mindset, our contemplations require another system of reference. In the top of the line distribution, The 7 Habits of Effective People, essayist Stephen Covey advanced the possibility of perspective changes. A worldview is positively a model or collection of reference where we see and comprehend the world. In the superb universe of weight the executives, dieting might be the social worldview where we attempt to control our pounds. A change in outlook is regularly a break with custom, with old methods for deduction, with matured ideal models. We should change our worldview to dismiss dieting; simply after that would we be able to make a solid sentimental association with dinners and our bodies.

While Covey's capacity is focused at the business network, he hits upon a worry that groups valid for interminable dieters. He accepts that people are much of the time attracted to treatment the issue without regard to the long haul ramifications of the "handy solution." He feels that this methodology really intensifies the issue rather than for all time understanding it. He factors to the physical body as a prized resource that every now and again is typically destroyed while one is for the most part on the challenge for quick results and momentary advantages. Recorded underneath are the means to begin your change in perspective of dismissing the dietary plan mindset.

Stage One: Recognize And Acknowledge The Harm That Dieting Causes

There exists a generous measure of learn about the damage that dieting causes. Recognize that the harm is genuine, and that kept dieting is just going to propagate your issues. A couple of the key undesirable impacts gathered from fundamental examinations are clarified beneath in two gatherings, enthusiastic and natural. As you read, have an individual stock, and have yourself which of the issues you as of now are encountering. Perceiving that dieting might be the issue can assist you with getting through the social fantasy that diets work. Keep in mind; if dieting might be the issue, how might it take part the solution?

Damage from Dieting: Biological and Health

Atlanta separate from lawyers century, starvation and human starvation have existed. Tragically, this is genuine at the present time. Natural selection recently structured endurance of the fattest-just individuals that have adequate vitality stores (abundance fat) could endure a starvation. Subsequently, our life structures are as yet equipped in this present day to battle starvation at the cell level. So far as the body can be included, dieting is a sort of starvation (regardless of the way that it's deliberate).

a. Chronic dieting encourages your body to hold more fat when you start eating once more. Low-calorie diets double the chemicals that produce and store fat in your body. This is a sort of organic remuneration to enable the body to store more vitality, or additional fat, subsequent to dieting.

b. Chronic dieting eases back the rate of weight loss with each progressive attempt to diet. It has been exhibited in both rodent and person contemplates.

c. Decrease digestion. Dieting triggers your body to turn out to be better at using calorie utilization by diminishing the body's reliance on vitality.

d. Boost gorges and yearnings. The two people and rodents have been demonstrated to indulge after constant food limitation. Food limitation invigorates the psyche to discharge a course of longings to expend more. After generous overabundance weight reduction, thinks about likewise show that rodents pick expending progressively fat, while people have been appeared to pick foods both immersed in fat and sugar.

e. Increase risk of untimely death toll and heart disease. A thirty-two-year study more prominent than 3,000 ladies and men in the Framingham Center Study has exhibited that regardless of starting pounds, individuals whose fat more than once rises and down-known as overabundance weight cycling or yo-yo dieting-have an expanded by and large demise check and double the standard danger of kicking the bucket of cardiovascular ailment. These outcomes had been free of cardiovascular hazard factors, and remained constant whether an individual was thin or hefty. The damage from yo-yo dieting may be equivalent to the dangers of remaining corpulent.

Correspondingly, results of the Harvard Alumni Health Study show that people who lose and gain at any rate eleven pounds inside ten years or somewhere in the vicinity, don't live inasmuch as the individuals who keep up a very much adjusted weight.

    f. Trigger satiety prompts to decay. Dieters for the most part quit eating because of a deliberate point of confinement rather than internal signs of totality. This, combined with skip-ping foods, can condition you to expend suppers of progressively greater size.

    g. Trigger body shape to change. Yo-yo dieters who consistently recapture the lost pounds will in general recover fat in the stomach region. This sort of fat stockpiling heightens the danger of cardiovascular illness.

Other written undesirable impacts incorporate cerebral pains, menstrual anomalies, exhaustion, dried out skin, and hair diminishing.

Damage from Dieting: Psychological and Emotional

Mental experts announced the following advertisement section impacts at the milestone 1992 National Institutes of Health, Excess weight reduction and Control Conference:

a. Dieting is related with eating issue. (Inside a disconnected research, dieters were eight events as prone to have issues with a benefiting from scatter by age fifteen, than non-dieters.)

b. Dieting could make pressure or help make the dieter progressively defenseless to its belongings. Autonomous of bodyweight itself, dieting is generally associated with feelings of fizzling, brought down confidence, and relational nervousness.

c. The dieter is much of the time helpless against decrease of control overeating while disregarding "the rules" of the dietary plan, regardless of whether there was a real or saw offense of the dietary plan. The unimportant view of expending a taboo suppers (independent of real calorie content) will do to bring about overeating. In another report, analysts David Garner and Susan Wooley present a convincing defense against the significant expense of bogus wish from dieting. They infer that:

d. Dieting consistently dissolves certainty and individual trust.

e. Many obese individuals expect they can't have become corpulent except if they had some basic character deficiency. Garner and Wooley contend that despite the fact that numerous corpulent individuals may encounter gorging and sadness, these psychological and social manifestations will be the aftereffect of dieting. Be that as it may, these overweight individuals effectively translate these indications as extra verification a basic issue. However, large individuals don't have extreme enthusiastic unsettling influences in contrast with ordinary weight individuals.

Stage 2: Be Familiar With Diet Mentality Characteristics And Thinking

The diet attitude regions in unobtrusive structures, despite the fact that you decide to dismiss dieting. It's fundamental that you perceive basic highlights of the dietary plan attitude; it will illuminate you on the off chance that you are as yet playing the dieting computer game. Disregard self discipline, getting respectful, and coming up short.

The general attributes of the way the dieter versus the non-dieter see eating, exercise, and improvement are outlined by a diagram beneath:

Disregard Willpower.

While just no specialist would anticipate that an individual should "will" blood flow strain to ordinary levels, specialists much of the time anticipate that their overweight individual should "will" their weight reduction by confining their food, as per Susan Z. Yanovski, M.D. That is additionally a predominant disposition among our clients and numerous Americans-all you will require is generally resolution and only a little restraint. In a 1993 Gallup Poll, the most run of the mill obstruction referred to thinning somewhere around women was determination.

For example, Marilyn is an amazingly fruitful lawyer who moved to the absolute best of the association stepping stool. She acknowledges her accomplishment for her commitment, resolve, and self-control. Be that as it may, when she endeavored to utilize these model ideas in her dieting endeavors, she bombed consistently. Whatever accomplishment she had achieved in her expert presence was dulled by her sentiment of coming up short with her eating.

For what reason was Marilyn in a situation to be in this manner taught in a solitary zone of her reality be that as it may, not in the extra? "Self-discipline" gets from the term follower. Identifying with Stephen Covey's work, on the off chance that you are a follower to your own profound qualities which have a superseding design, all things considered, you'll have the will to move them out. Marilyn thought profoundly that creating demanding understandings and keeping perfect data had been necessities to building self-assurance with her clients and her legal counselor. In any case, some way or another, hearing that bread wasn't right utilizing one diet plan and anything with sugars was off base on another, didn't incite a similar kind of profound convictions. Attempt as she may, she couldn't generally feel that chocolate chip treats had been that insidious!

Self control can be disclosed as a push to counter characteristic wishes and supplant them with proscriptive rules. It additionally suggests the ability to do terrible employments that aren't basic.

The longing to have desserts is common, standard, and very agreeable! Any diet that tells you that you can't have desserts is absolutely conflicting with your natural want. The dietary plan be-comes a few inflexible rules, and these sorts of rules can just barely trigger insubordination.

Self control won't have a place in Intuitive Feeding on. As Marilyn turned into an Intuitive Eater, she found that meeting her own pointers fortified her natural senses, than countering them rather. She had no one else's proscriptive standards to follow or to oppose. Marilyn has stopped battling the ghost self discipline battle and has delivered harmony with suppers and her body.

Disregard Being Obedient

A good natured recommendation by a life partner or life partner such as: "Honey, you should have the seared chicken... "Or "You shouldn't eat those fries... ", can set off an inward food resistance. In this sort of food battle, your only weapons store to battle turns into a twofold order of fries. We call this "overlooks you eating."

In material science, opposition consistently happens as a response to constrain. We see this hypothesis doing his thing in the public eye revolts as often as possible emits when the weight of power becomes also incredible. Likewise, the simple demonstration to be advised how to continue (really if it's something you ought to do), can bring about a defiant chain reaction. Precisely like "horrible two-year-olds" or teenagers who revolt to show they are autonomous, dieters can start defiant eating in light of the make a move of dieting, utilizing its gathering of unbending standards. In this way, it's not stunning to tune in to from our clients that breaking the rules of a diet plan make them feel like they did on the off chance that they were rebellious youngsters. Yet, take focus, resistance is a standard work of self-protection shielding your space, or individual limits.

Think about an individual limit as a high block fence encompassing you, with just 1 entryway. Just you can open up that entryway, if you pick. Thusly, no one is permitted inside, except if you welcome the person in. Inside your fence dwell individual feelings, musings, and organic pointers.

People who expect they comprehend the thing you require and advise you how to continue are choosing the lock to your door, or attacking your limits. Keep in mind; no one might be the expert of "you." Just you know your thoughts, emotions, and encounters. No one might comprehend what's inside, except if he is told by you, by welcoming him in. What diet or diet plan advocate may potentially know whether you are starving or exactly what amount of food it will require to fulfill you? How would anybody yet you know very well what surface and flavor sensations will get satisfying to your sense of taste? In the brilliant universe of dieting, individual limits are crossed at numerous sums. For example, you are determined what things to eat, exactly its amount to expend, and when to eat it. These choices should all wind up being close to home decisions, with deference for explicit self-rule and body markers. While food direction will originate from somewhere else, you ought to in the long run be responsible for the when, what, and exactly the amount of eating.

Disregard Failure.

Our incessant dieters head into our workplaces feeling just as they are disappointments. Regardless of whether they are profoundly situated administrators, conspicuous whizzes, or straight-An understudy, every one of them talk about their food experiences despicably, and they question whether they'll ever be able to feel effective in the area of eating. The dietary plan attitude strengthens feelings of progress or coming up short. You can't fall flat at Intuitive Eating-it's a learning strategy at each point in transit. What used to become viewed as a mishap will rather be viewed as an ascent experience. You'll get back progressing nicely when you watch this as progress, not disappointment.

Stage 3: Eliminate The Dieter's Tools

The dieter relies upon outer powers to adjust his eating, staying with a controlled diet, eating since now is the ideal time, or eating just a predetermined (and estimated) sum, regardless of whether hungry or not. The dieter additionally approves progress by outside powers, the scale principally, asking, "Exactly what number of pounds have I lost?" "Is my abundance weight up or down?" It is period to dispose of your dieting devices. Dispose of the feast programs and the suppers and restroom scales.

On the off chance that all it required was a magnificent "reasonable" calorie-confined dinner expect to shed pounds, we'd be viewed as a country of thin human free feast plans are ample from magazines, papers, the Internet, and even some food organizations.

Stage 4: Become Compassionate Toward Yourself

At the point when the world about you is dieting, and euphoric about how precisely weight is dissolving off subsequently of the most recent diet plan fever it's reasonable that you could get pulled in. Be that as it may, this draw is generally significantly something beyond style.

In her distribution, The Religion of Thinness, Harvard-prepared scholar and researcher, Michelle M. Lelwica makes a convincing contention about how precisely the unending mission for slenderness, through dieting, satisfies an otherworldly food desires. The journey for dieting goes about as a "biggest reason" by:

a. Providing two or three fantasies to accept about the "benefits" of slimness.
b. Giving ceremonies to organize the everyday lives of women.
c. Creating an ethical code which to live and eat by.
d. Creating a typical relationship and a network for females.

Considering these secret "benefits" of dieting, just no big surprise you may get tempted by the "benefits" of dieting. Try not to overcome yourself okay with intriguing dreams of attempting one more diet or simply endeavoring to diet. It requires some investment to disregard this craving, despite the fact that you mentally under-stand that the journey for dieting is really vain.

Adapt Together to your Emotions without requiring Food

Discover approaches to solace and straightforwardness, support, divert, and fathom your issues without requiring food. Stress, forlornness, fatigue, and outrage are sentiments the greater part of us experience all through presence. Everyone has its trigger and every offer its very own mollification. Suppers won't fix these sentiments. It could comfort for the present moment, divert from the uneasiness, or really numb you directly into a food headache. Be that as it may, food won't resolve the issue.

On the off chance that anything, eating for a passionate craving is just going to make you feel more terrible after some time. You'll in the long run need to adapt to the wellspring of the feeling, alongside the distress of overeating.

Benefiting from doesn't happen in a void. Of your weight in any case, food generally has mental affiliations. In the event that you have any uncertainty, catch a look at supper's advertisements. They drive our eating catches not so much through our stomachs yet through the mental association. They suggest in sixty negligible seconds or less you may:

a. Capture sentiment with a sentimental mug of espresso/coffee

b. Bake somebody glad.

c. Incentive yourself with an affluent treat.

Eating can be one of the most genuinely loaded experiences that we have in our lives. The mental mood to expending is characterized from the principal day time that the newborn child develops the bosoms or the container to suppress his crying. It's at that point fortified at whatever points a treat rises to relieve a scratched knee, or frozen yogurt is normally eaten to celebrate only a youth baseball triumph. Almost every culture and religion utilizes food as a fundamental representative custom, from the American Thanksgiving blowout to the Jewish Passover Seder. At whatever point a critical life experience is praised with dinners, the mental association develops, from the I-got-the -advancement-ner extraordinary occasion to the yearly birthday cake. Moreover, each time food is used for a little twisted licking or solace, the enthusiastic relationship reinforces.

Food is love, dinners are comfort, suppers are prize, and dinners are a confided in companion. What's more, some of the time, food turns into your solitary companion in events of agony and dejection. The eating experience itself, overeating particularly, inspires sentiments, and the ones emotions have any kind of effect your ability to eat typically. Likely the most hindering feelings that overeating can stir up are blame and disgrace. Studies have exhibited that in spite of the fact that you may have prompt passionate solace from eating, the negative rush of blame that blasts forward is ground-breaking a lot of to totally dispose of the alleviation.

If you supplant the blame with feelings of self-sympathy, you'll become liberated to concentrate on your basic issues and discover techniques to get them and adapt to them.

Getting an Intuitive Eater implies seeing how to wind up being delicate with yourself about how precisely you use dinners to arrangement, and letting continue of the blame. As odd as this would sound, eating may have been the simply way of dealing with stress you'd to finish troublesome events in your day by day life. It might in like manner have been an unavoidable outcome of long periods of dieting and feelings of hardship and gloom that emerged from dieting. Dieting itself can bring about feelings, which at last outcome in utilizing food to deal with these sentiments chalks up another horrible everyday practice because of dieting.

The Continuum Of Emotional Eating

Food can be used to deal with sentiments in a variety of ways. Utilizing food as such isn't a component of organic appetite, however of passionate food yearnings. Enthusiastic eating is unquestionably activated by emotions, such as weariness or outrage, not by food desires. These sentiments can bring about anything from a kind snack to a crazy gorge. It's fundamental that you perceive that this adapting framework lies on a continuum of solidarity that starts toward one side with moderate, practically general tactile expending despite what might be expected end with desensitizing, anesthetizing eating regularly.

Raising an Intuitive Eater: What Works together with Kids and Teens

We will in general be inquired as to whether it's conceivable to train youngsters Intuitive Eating. The appropriate response isn't simply can you truly assist youngsters with returning to the Intuitive Eaters these were during childbirth, in any case it is frequently less troublesome than with grown-ups. Kids are significantly less questionable than grown-ups and much increasingly open and anxious.

How about we start with avoidance. At the point when a kid is conceived, this kid has the inborn capacity had a need to see how to eat.

I was fortunately enough as of late to go to a companion's little girl, who had essentially conceived an offspring fourteen days before to her wonderful child young lady. Alexis was just getting increasingly alright with the staggering errand of deciding what to look like after her new conceived. Which cry planned that she was lethargic, which said that there is a diaper that necessary changing, and which let her comprehend that the infant had a need to eat? Presently, in the event that you've at any point watched a destitute child; you comprehend that her most unmistakable cry might be the one of food longings. On the off chance that the child is neglected when she's ravenous, she'll shout and shout until gave the bosoms or jug.

The yearning signal is intensely intended for about all infants, and there exists a characteristic nature to help make the reliance on sustenance known. I was situated and talking with Alexis, when little Lily made the sounds that let her mother comprehend that she was starving. To sit watching this dazzling association among mother and kid was a real blessing. Lily breast fed utilizing one bosom and the other, so when she was finished, she dismissed her important head and nodded off. Alexis was in amazement of how intuitive her newborn child's eating experience was.

In the event that there is attunement to the wide cluster of obvious and nuanced messages that the kid offers, the child will grow up with a sentiment of self-self-assurance that his needs work and will be normally met. At the point when the child is hungry and is typically immediately encouraged, numerous significant correspondences will become passed on. The first message is that food desires is an all regular, ordinary, and "right" sensation. Later on, the impression of food desires will be related to the movement to discover food. An adjusted reaction to the kid's food longings will evoke a sentiment of security, taking out any worry with hardship. In the event that, rather, this essential need of the youngster isn't met at the right occasions, the kid will begin to expect that there won't be sufficient food. Accordingly, this child is in danger of quieting hunger signals, rather than believing that the food desires signal is a confided in message all through life.

Envision a newborn child whose set on an encouraging everyday practice, a thing that was a typical proposal from ages later. The mother or father was encouraged to put the newborn child on an everyday practice of eating, which go from each 2-3 hours to each 3 to 4 hours. Numerous guardians reacted emphatically to the proposal, as managing the eating plan enables them to plan throughout the day consistently ahead of time. Of program, most guardians didn't receive this system out of egotistical requires. These were advised a customary sustaining timetable will be best for the child.

Lamentably, this is basically not for the most part the situation, as this technique gets the possibility to make various issues. On the off chance that the child got starving and cried around 30 minutes before the booked time, the mother or father was provoked to keep down to sustain her. Assuming, be that as it may, the child wasn't yet starving right now, she might be cajoled to eat at any rate. Since craving and completion signals were not normally being strengthened, the destitute, shouting child or the not so much yet starving infant was on his strategy to doubting these powerful messages. For the destitute baby, the potential worry with future hardship may flourish. For the infant who was propelled to eat before food desires had adequately shown up, false impressions and protection from benefiting from can develop. For a youngster who was basically benefited from plan, than on request somewhat, moving to the baby years can start a confused sentimental association with food. On the off chance that a decent measure of food gets open to a youngster who encountered a feeling of hardship earliest stages, the kid could be inclined to build up a characteristic propensity to indulge. At the point when another feast is offered, 1 of 2 potential outcomes may happen. The youngster might just be excessively finished and won't eat or may surpass this totality transmission and take in much more suppers, amassing for another potential starvation. For the child who was just persuaded to expend as a newborn child, the opportunity to eat much more autonomously as a baby may likewise introduce two potential outcomes. He may proceed relentlessly to expend when he's not yet starving, or he could apply his autonomy by declining to eat.

Luckily, today encouraging calendars are once in a while prescribed, and upright parental figures tend to react habitually to the youngster's appetite signals. Be that as it may, shouldn't something be said about signs totality? Have you at any point truly attempted to keep to encourage a youngster after she dismisses her psyche from the bosoms or jug, since you're terrified that she lacks sustenance or that she's not so much developing rapidly a lot of? At the point when that youngster's belly is unquestionably full, she will typically recoil from turning out to be coercively fed. We've seen, with loathsomeness, little children who were oftentimes convinced to eat much more than they required, all through their underlying couple of years.

At last they either put on significantly more abundance weight than was empowering or wound up participating in dinners battles and would not expend particularly by any stretch of the imagination. For example, the mother of an amazingly youthful customer was in certainty portrayed youngster defensive arrangements by the specialist stirred up in treatment. This mother had procured a sister who experienced died in a starved condition from anorexia nervosa. Because of this, she related getting underweight with death toll and became alarmed that her child will be underweight. As an all out outcome, she stuffed her little kid with enormous quantities of food. This is seen as enthusiastic kid misuse.

The most essential piece of guaranteeing that a child holds the greater part of his intrinsic capacity around craving and completion is trust. Ellyn Satter, in her weighty book, Child of Mine: Feeding with Like and Good Sense (2000), relevantly says that it's the guardians' business to supply the dinners, and the youngster's work to expend to such an extent or short of what he prerequisites. In early stages, it's occasional a parent veers off out of this give and consider, however as youngsters re-situate of the "milk simply" arrange, guardians have an undeniably increasingly troublesome period staying tuned legitimately into a kid's eating markers. Guardians believe that there are along these lines many "authentic" known explanations behind them to endeavor to deal with the kid's expending. In this time of the plague of youth weight issues, the fear of a child putting on an inordinate measure of weight regularly prospects good natured pediatricians to give guardians the direction to watch what and how especially a child is eating.

The contrary circumstance may likewise be available, when there is a fear that the child isn't putting on enough weight. Moreover, numerous guardians who wish to enable their children to be as solid since they can empower them to eat just healthfully dense foods and restrict them from play suppers. In spite of the fact that this attempt to control the aggregate sum and sort of food kids are eating is regularly conceived from extraordinary goals, what's more, it brings the possibility of the child's question of his signs. Not just are his food longings and completion markers missed, yet additionally his intrinsic under-standing up of his food decisions and how his body appears to be subsequent to eating various amounts and sorts of food sources. As opposed to hearing and regarding her own physical responses to the eating experience, the child responds to the mother or father's outer message, rather than her very own inner comprehension. This response can have immense varieties to be the "acceptable little woman" and performing everything that Mommy wants, to performing out as the insubordinate child, who won't eat most, everything.

The Science and Psychology of Intuitive Eating

Imagine a reality where you woke up every day and had a basic association with food. You ate when you were hungry and stopped when you were full. There are no events other than a picnic for you. Do not be defeated when you have eaten something "terrible". There is simply no shame or guilt. Don't eat out of anger or misery. You just ate what felt solid and your body. In spite of prevalent thinking, this isn't a story book. This sort of association with dinners is most likely conceivable. Suppose you realized that you had a need to do to get it going was to trust - trust the body and you to at last make educated alternatives encompassing food?

Trust is the middle purpose of a dietary way of thinking alluded to as Intuitive Taking in. It's by creating depending upon your body's interior signs in regards to food yearnings and totality that you could start to make extraordinary decisions around eating. You can recognize physical and mental yearnings and over the long haul you'll see that you could eat in a way that enables you to find your characteristic abundance weight and health.

This methodology is clearly not equivalent to what we typically hear. No more does great medical coverage and regular pounds require diet programs, calorie limitation, and exceptional exercise. A remarkable opposite, the simple demonstration of hearing the body, believing its insight and respecting its prerequisites can bring about weight decrease, improved vitality and a greatly improved encounter of life. In case you're keen on this methodology, recorded beneath are 4 significant bits of knowledge in to the science and the brain research of Intuitive Eating and exactly why it truly works:

There is a Brain in your Belly

The information behind eating intuitively is in truth situated in science. Have you at any point persevered through a "feeling" that something had not been correct? Maybe you have felt "off" utilizing conditions? Felt butterflies in your paunch? Or on the other hand encountered an annoyed mid-region when needing to deal with a situation you encountered uncertain about? That is your bodies enteric on edge framework talking, generally alluded to as the "gut-mind." Yes, we do have a brain inside our tummy. Our "gut-brain," of program, contrasts from the brain in our psyche. The enteric apprehensive program is really housed underneath the mucosal covering and between your strong layers of the throat, the stomach, and the little and internal organs. Through an extraordinarily complex system of neurons and neuro-synthetic compounds; authorizes and controls events in different regions of the body, similar to the brain itself. Specialists have confirmed that the enteric sensory system is consistently giving data to your minds in regards to our dietary necessities. The greater part of us make sense of how to eat by hearing messages originating from past ourselves - correspondences from our folks, educators, companions, or the press. Eating intuitively needs respecting the messages from your internal method to acquire knowing to support you.

Your Body Comprehends when it's Hungry and when it truly is Full.

Starting the technique of seeing how to trust your "gut-mind" and your body framework shrewdness implies understanding your body's internal signs concerning yearning and completion. It's imperative to such an extent that you decelerate and watch with the goal that you can hear what the body is stating. Periodically, we're moving in this manner rapidly through the globe that individuals spend our period separated from the body. We run in one gathering to another, skip suppers at whatever point we don't have period, or indulge before a day's over. This separation unleashes destruction on our pace of digestion and on our euphoria. On the off chance that you begin to tune into the body, you'll perceive what it feels as if when you're hungry and full. Your body will tell you when you're exhausted or vigorous or experiencing issues processing. Watch your body's messages.

How would you experience when you're ravenous? Will your stomach experience light and rumble? Do you get yourself slight cerebral pains or does the mouth territory start to water? Notice on the off chance that you are starting to feel full. Where do you feeling it inside your body? In your belly? Do you start to unwind or inhale less troublesome? Everybody is extraordinary; subsequently we'll all have our own special real sensations and instant messages. You have to time to ask the body what it needs. Check out the vibes of food desires and totality and you'll be en route to eating intuitively.

Believing The Body Benefits Your Health From Multiple Ways

Probably the greatest blessing you may get from benefiting from intuitively is the capacity to confide in both the body and yourself. This may have significant advantages without anyone else generally speaking health. Obviously, everybody comprehends that pressure is hard for our health. Washing ourselves in strain hormones consistently makes it hard to lose overabundance weight and assemble muscle. It can cause depletion and debilitate invulnerability. Be that as it may, believing your body's inward prompts and feeling guaranteed in this methodology empowers you to loosen up into your sentimental association with food in addition to your reality. Envision the stream straight down impact this may have without anyone else generally speaking admirably turning out to be. Trusting and getting the expert on yourself just as your very own needs can make you are feeling progressively engaged to cause an actual existence where you too can truly flourish.

By putting trust in yourself you may start to feel more secure in your connections and on the planet. You may find that you can move away from being no picnic for yourself to being increasingly caring. From that point, self-judgment around food can turn into a relic of past times. Kindly don't disparage the intensity of setting trust in your body and yourself.

Health and Well-Being

Positive health brain science speaks to the requests subterranean insect end of enthusiastic states, which incorporate inclination perky, glad, thankful, and has been appeared by a few examinations to foresee future degrees of health and prosperity. In addition, these impacts amass and compound after some time, making individuals more beneficial, all the more socially coordinated, powerful, and versatile. Additionally, there are reported physical medical advantages of such states, which incorporate lower levels of the pressure chemical cortisol and less aggravation. An investigation by Tylka and Wilcox (2006) on 340 school ladies demonstrated that two center develops of Intuitive Eating, (1) eating for physical instead of passionate reasons and (2) dependence on inner craving and satiety signals to decide when and the amount to eat, exceptionally adds to the mental prosperity including: idealism, mental solidness (a pointer of strength, or the capacity to recoup from affliction), genuine self-respect, beneficial outcome, proactive adapting, and social critical thinking.

The examination's discoveries feature the significance of an individual's capacity to identify and take care of their feelings and their organic prompts of craving and satiety, as location and consciousness of these states are particularly associated with prosperity. These discoveries approve a significant number of the Intuitive Eating standards (Honor Your Hunger, Respect Your Fullness, Coping with Feelings without Using Food, Reject the Diet Mentality).

Intuitive Eating Holds Promise for U.S. Military

The U.S. Armed force led a promising pilot study on the benefits of Intuitive Eating for its soldiers (Heilson and Cole 2011). Analysts from the U.S. Armed force Baylor graduate program in sustenance assessed both inspirations for eating and the Intuitive Eating qualities of one hundred dynamic obligation military assistance individuals matured eighteen to sixty-five years of age. The outcomes showed that military assistance individuals with an ordinary weight file scored the most noteworthy on the Intuitive Eating Scale, were bound to eat for physical reasons, and depended upon their inner craving satiety signs, while members with better than average weight record levels were slanted to eat for non-intuitive or nonphysical reasons. In view of these promising outcomes, a bigger report is in progress, which will assess the viability of an Intuitive Eating system to help break the enthusiastic, ecological, and social association with eating in the military assistance.

Self-Silencing

Self-silencing is the concealment of one's contemplations, emotions, or necessities and it is a sexual orientation marvel affecting ladies' psychological wellness. The procedure of self-quieting is thought to start in youthfulness, a defenseless time when body disappointment and social weights develop. While quieting their voices, young ladies may start to disregard or smother physiological or hunger signals that are conflicting with cultural thoughts of slenderness. Articulation of considerations, emotions, or necessities seems, by all accounts, to be a basic part of smart dieting practices. Shouse and Nilsson (2011) assessed the connection between disarranged eating, Intuitive Eating, and self-hushing and found that Intuitive Eating is amplified when a lady has elevated levels of enthusiastic mindfulness, joined with low degrees of self-quieting.

Nonetheless, when high passionate mindfulness was combined with increasingly self-quieting, members had progressively confused eating and less Intuitive Eating. The scientists accept that when ladies have clearness about their musings and sentiments, yet quietness their voices, hunger signs may get befuddled, which may diminish trust of inward signals of craving and satiation. The most intuitive and least disarranged eaters in the examination showed high passionate mindfulness and low self-quieting. The aftereffects of this investigation approve the standards: Challenge the Food Police and Cope with Your Emotions without Using Food.

ACKNOWLEDGMENT AND BODY APPRECIATION

While the capacity to eat intuitively is innate, the probability of staying an Intuitive Eater is affected by the earth, which incorporates family, companions, and culture. Intuitive Eating can be obstructed by a situation that needs acknowledgment as well as forces inflexible standards for eating that disregard an individual's internal encounter, (for example, appetite or fulfillment). Moreover, when individuals urge others to be incredulous of their bodies, they (ladies particularly) figure out how to eat in a separated way trying to control their appearance, rather than tuning in to their bodies. Also, strain to get in shape by relatives, companions, and culture (in lieu of body acknowledgment) adds to concentrating on appearance-related eating. Numerous individuals are shocked to discover that body praises can be a type of making a decision about an individual by their appearance, for example, "You look extraordinary—how much weight did you lose?" or "I wish I had a body like yours."

Acceptance Model of Intuitive Eating

A progression of concentrates by Tracy Tylka and associates (Avalos and Tylka 2006, Augustus-Horvath and Tylka 2011), on almost 600 school ladies and 800 ladies ages eighteen to sixty-five years of age, individually, found that putting accentuation on body capacity and body thankfulness are key approaches to make an interpretation of body acknowledgment into Intuitive Eating practices.

At the point when ladies stress the usefulness of their bodies over appearance, they are increasingly disposed to eat as indicated by their body's organic prompts. Besides, they found that receiving a mentality of body gratefulness anticipated Intuitive Eating, in light of the fact that good body frames of mind are related with more prominent attention to body signals, joined with a more noteworthy inclination to respect these signs. Their examination demonstrates that it is imperative to advance a positive body direction, which centers on body gratefulness and body usefulness, as opposed to appearance, which thusly, encourages Intuitive Eating. Tylka and partners found that body gratefulness was remarkably and decidedly identified with Intuitive Eating in a wide assortment of age bunches for ladies. They distinguished four signs of body appreciation:

1. Having a positive assessment of the body in spite of size and saw blemishes.

2. Monitoring and mindful to the body's needs.

3. Taking part in sound practices to deal with the body.

4. Securing the body by dismissing ridiculous media body beliefs.

Tylka and partners accept that it is essential to challenge Western declaration of the meager perfect generalization and advance acknowledgment of an assorted variety of body sizes.

Culture Acceptance

An entrancing arrangement of multi-social investigations by Hawks and associates demonstrate that before and during the beginning times of westernization, people from their local nations are normal Intuitive Eaters, yet this procedure of eating is relinquished to the detriment of the westernized flimsy perfect (Hawks et al. 2004b, Madanat and Hawks 2004).

During cultural assimilation, the westernized standard of excellence becomes disguised, by means of the assault of unreasonable media pictures of slimness, and indigenous

Intuitive Eating styles dissolve away, toward outer signals of eating, the two of which can prompt stoutness and eating issue. These acknowledgments examines bolster and approve Principle 7—Respect Your Body.

Shouldn't something be said about Men? A significant number of the Intuitive Eating examines have been directed on ladies or on blended gatherings of people, yet not men as it were. There are considers in progress investigating Intuitive Eating issues in men. A fundamental report on 181 school men by Gast and partners (in press) found that men scoring high on the Hawks' Intuitive Eating Scale were related with a lower weight list, contrasted with men with low Intuitive Eating scores. The men likewise set more an incentive on being physically fit and sound, as opposed to on a perfect weight. The scientists recommended that Intuitive Eating appears to be obviously appropriate for men since it expands on men's enemy of dieting sees (men regularly see dieting practices as ladylike), and expands on self-care wellness convictions that have all the earmarks of being almost certain held by men.

INTUITIVE Eating is a Lifestyle:

Figuring out how to tune in to your body and regard your its astuteness is definitely not a stylish dieting approach like others that have traveled every which way throughout the years. Or maybe, eating intuitively is a methodology that can turn into a natural piece of your life. The ideas are basic yet significantly ground-breaking when put to utilize.

As intuitive eating is training and a lifestyle, as opposed to a pre-set dinner plan that you essentially need to hold fast to, it's not 100 percent precise constantly. A few days you may think that its simple to tune in to your body's internal signals. Different days it might be all the more a battle. Yet, as you work on tuning in, the whole methodology will come all the more effectively and be increasingly reliable after some time. What's more, the advantages as far as self-information, genuine feelings of serenity, and ideal health will be significantly broader than anything you can understand from a common weight reduction diet.

Here, we love educating about eating intuitively. We accept unequivocally that nobody find out about you than YOU. So as you consider all the data out there with respect to food and health make a stride back and look inside. You have such a large amount of the data you need inside your very own body. Your activity is just to work on tuning in.

Conclusion

These rules condense the parts of this book. The request where they're introduced isn't a flat out, similarly as nothing in this book is outright, aside from surrendering the quest for dieting. Use them as your formula card, as we recommended toward the starting as far as possible of this book. Be that as it may, similarly as you may extemporize in cooking your dish from the composed formula, be imaginative with these rules. Use what feels directly for you, add to them on the off chance that you like, and dispose of what doesn't fit. The main concern is to confide in your gut—utilize your intuitive abilities to feel great with eating and to discharge yourself from the jail of dieting.

Step by Step Guidelines

In case you're somebody who cooks, you'll realize that before you figured out how to cook, simply pulling out a formula card may have made you feel on edge about whether the completed mixture could ever look like any cooked dish you'd at any point before observed. So as to increase a solace level in your kitchen, you most likely expected to see a portion of the essential ideas of cooking. In the event that the formula said "stew," you wouldn't have realized the contrast between bubbling, stewing, or sautéing. The accompanying rules are like your formula card. In the event that you take a gander at them before you read the remainder of the book, you may get confounded and misconstrue the motivation behind each. When you've gotten settled with the Intuitive Eating reasoning, how-ever, these rules can turn into a snappy and simple reference when you have to reconnect with the procedure.

Stage 1—PRINCIPLE ONE: REJECT THE DIET MENTALITY

Toss out the diet books and magazine articles that offer you bogus any desire for shedding pounds rapidly, effectively, and for all time. Take advantage of the lies that led you to feel disappointed every time another diet stops working and you regain your full weight. In the event that you permit even one little would like to wait that another and better diet may be hiding around the bend, it will keep you from being allowed to rediscover Intuitive Eating.

1. Make a solid duty to quit any pretense of dieting for an amazing remainder. For whatever length of time that you clutch even the smallest idea, guarantee, or expectation that dieting is in your future, you will undermine your capacity to turn into an Intuitive Eater.

2. Toss out the entirety of your calorie counters and old diet books and articles.

3. At the point when companions talk about the most current prevailing fashion diet or you see a TV ad or magazine article on dieting—abstain from getting brought into the fervor that may emerge. Rather, take a full breath and tenderly guarantee yourself that you are focused on

another perspective and feeling about food and eating, and that dieting isn't a piece of this new procedure.

4. Ensure your food limits by declining to enable others to mention to you what to eat, when to eat, or the amount to eat. Secure your body limits by declining to enable others to offer remarks about your weight and body. 5. In the event that you notice that you're feeling defiant or starting to eat unwittingly, check in with yourself to check whether regardless you're clutching diet thinking and diet decides that are setting off this response or in case you're being assaulted by any outside limit intruders.

Stage 2—PRINCIPLE TWO: HONOR YOUR HUNGER

Keep your body organically bolstered with satisfactory vitality and sugars. Else you can trigger a base drive to indulge. When you arrive right now of inordinate craving, all expectations of moderate, cognizant eating are brief and unessential. Figuring out how to respect this first natural sign makes way for re-building trust with yourself and food.

1. Start to tune in to the littlest commotion or feeling that shows that you are encountering hunger, for example, a snarling or protesting stomach, a slight migraine, an absence of mental center, crankiness, absence of vitality, and so forth.

2. When you perceive your natural appetite, make an opportunity to eat.

3. In the event that you disregard this most fundamental flag and get over hungry, it will be extremely difficult to recognize what you truly need to eat or when you've had enough. Test with starting to eat at around a "3" or "4" on the "Craving Discovery Scale."

4. In the event that you don't appear to encounter hunger flags over significant stretches of time, you should take a stab at eating each three to four hours. In the end, your body will become acclimated to being nourished normally and will start to give you trustworthy yearning signals.

5. Remember that in the event that you are debilitated or focused on, hunger signs might be blunted. It's critical to sustain your body on those days, as well, regardless of whether you don't feel the appetite.

6. Be readied—make certain to set aside a few minutes for shop-ping for food, concocting or picking premade food, and for social occasion snacks or even suppers to place in a lunch pack or to convey in the vehicle. Along these lines, you show regard for your body's signs and can accommodate your needs.

Stage 3—PRINCIPLE THREE: MAKE PEACE WITH FOOD

Call a détente, stop the food battle! Give yourself un-contingent authorization to eat. In the event that you disclose to yourself that you can't or shouldn't have a specific food, it can prompt serious sentiments of hardship that incorporate with wild desires and, regularly, gorging. At the point when you at last "yield" to your taboo food, eating will be knowledgeable about such power; it for the most part brings about Last Supper overeating, and overpowering blame.

1. Give yourself unrestricted consent to eat whatever you truly like. Make avocado sincerely equal to lettuce and peach pie comparable to a peach.

2. Be careful with giving yourself "pseudo-authorization" by disclosing to yourself that you can eat what you like, however proceeding to hold blameworthy contemplations about your food decisions. It won't work!

3. Try not to deny yourself of any food that sounds engaging you.

4. See how your body feels when eating this food and that it is so fulfilling to your tongue. Give careful consideration of these encounters for your memory bank.

5. Keep a plentiful stockpile of the considerable number of foods that you figure you may get a kick out of the chance to eat. (Restock the sup-employ when it gets low.)

Stage 4—PRINCIPLE FOUR: CHALLENGE THE FOOD POLICE

Shout a boisterous "NO" to considerations in your mind that pronounce you're "acceptable" for eating negligible calories or "awful" on the grounds that you ate a bit of chocolate cake. The Food Police screen the irrational principles that dieting has made. The police headquarters is housed somewhere down in your mind, and its amplifier yells negative thorns, miserable expressions, and blame inciting arraignments. Pursuing the Food Police away is a basic advance in coming back to Intuitive Eating.

1. Distinguish your mutilated food, dieting, and eating considerations and convictions. Toss them out and supplant them with reality.

2. Tune in for the damaging voices which can talk unsafe considerations:

a. The Food Police voice is brutal and basic and is driven by the dieting mindset. It very well may be animated by tuning in to the media, guardians, and friends. It keeps you at war with your association with food and your body.

b. The Nutrition Informant voice is critical and intrigues with the Food Police. It gives you sustenance actualities to help legitimize your dieting.

c. The Diet Rebel voice is irate and is conceived because of limit intruders who traverse the line into the private space that holds your Intuitive Eating signs and emotions about your body. It secures your self-rule while additionally causing some ruinous eating conduct.

3. Build up the accommodating voices that can get you through harsh occasions and make your eating relationship increasingly agreeable:

a. The Food Anthropologist: voice portrays impartial perceptions. It takes note of your considerations and activities as for your food world to assist you with settling on decisions about what you need to eat, when you need to eat, and the amount you have to eat. It can likewise record these musings in your memory bank, so they will be effectively open when required later on to assist you with settling on eating choices.

b. The Nurturer: voice is delicate and delicate and gives calming and consoling articulations that help you through this procedure.

c. The Rebel Ally: voice advances from the Diet Rebel voice and encourages you secure your limits against any individual who attacks your eating space.

d. The Nutrition Ally voice replaces the Nutrition Informant voice when the Food Police are ousted. It is keen on good dieting with no concealed dieting motivation.

The Intuitive Eater voice addresses your gut responses. You were brought into the world with this voice, and it offers you messages and responses about your eating that no one but you can know. It additionally causes you settle on choices that lone you reserve the option to make.

4. Watch out for negative self-talk dependent on the accompanying silly convictions and contorted reasoning:

a. Dichotomous intuition—thinking in a win or bust, high contrast design.

b. Absolutist reasoning—magical thinking that accepts that one conduct will completely influence and control a subsequent conduct.

c. Catastrophic intuition—thinking in misrepresented ways.

d. Pessimistic reasoning — where a given circumstance is found in its most dire outcome imaginable.

e. Linear deduction—thinking in a straight line, taking into consideration no factors, concentrating on the final products.

5. Supplant negative self-chat with positive self-talk dependent on balanced reasoning. A few instances of objective reasoning include:

a. Living in the dim—moderate considerations, not highly contrasting.

b. Permissive considerations and articulations.

c. Accurate, non-overstated considerations.

d. Process thinking—center on consistent change and getting the hang of, organizing the methods as opposed as far as possible.

Stage 5: PRINCIPLE FIVE: FEEL YOUR PLENITY

Tune the body flags that reveal that you will never be anxious again. Observe the signs indicating that it is easily refillable. Relax during a party or meal and ask yourself how you know the food and what your current level of completion is.

1. Focus on your completion signals. However, recollect, the main way that you can do this is to give yourself unequivocal consent to eat. You should immovably accept that you will have the option to eat again when you get eager so as to have the option to stop when you're full.

2. Make certain to respect your craving. In case you're eager for over, your desperation to eat will make extraordinary trouble in perceiving your completion signals. Similarly, in the event that you start eating before obvious craving emerges, your totality signs will be quieted—you're probably going to be guided by your tongue rather than your stomach.

3. Dispose of the thought that you should complete everything on your plate since you dread squandering food. Unmistakably more harm should be possible to your body and your mind by eating additional food than by disposing

of it.

4. Increment your awareness so as to assist you with recognizing satiety.

    a. Try eating without interruption so you can be completely present during your supper.

    b. Pause in a feast or tidbit and take an opportunity to check your completion level. This isn't a pledge to quit eating yet a promise to check in with your body and taste buds.

Take a taste check. Ask, "How does the food taste? Does it live up to your desires? Is it fulfilling your taste buds? Or on the other hand would you say you are proceeding to eat in light of the fact that it's there?"

Take a satiety check. Focus on the signs that your stomach offers you to demonstrate that you're turning out to be comfortably full. Ask, "What's my appetite or completion level? Am I still eager? Is hunger leaving? Do I feel voracious? Am I starting to feel fulfilled?"

    c. Identify the Last Bite Threshold. This is the endpoint. You realize that the nibble of food in your mouth is the last. Try not to stress on the off chance that you can't do this from the start—it will at last become intuitive. On the off chance that you feel disillusioned that you need to stop now, recollect, you can eat this food or food once more, when your appetite returns. Eating is in reality all the more fulfilling when you're serenely eager, as opposed to effectively full. You're giving yourself a blessing by halting at this point.

d. Make a solid explanation to yourself that you've arrived at the limit chomp by putting your fork and blade on your plate or by pushing your plate ahead a smidgen.

e. Give your remains to the server to wrap up in case you're at a café or placed them in the fridge in case you're at home.

f. Say, "No, thank you" immovably to your host or entertainer if more food is being pushed onto you. You reserve an option to state "no."

5. Ensure that you have a lot of food profit capable for your suppers. In the event that you give yourself too little to even think about eating, you'll never feel fulfilled or full. You don't require "to an extreme" food, yet "excessively little" food will attack this procedure.

6. Select foods that have some substance. On the off chance that you just pick "air foods, for example, rice cakes and crude vegetables, you'll get a misguided feeling of satiety, just to get eager again far and away too rapidly. Feed yourself "genuine food."

Stage 6—PRINCIPLE SIX: DISCOVER THE SATISFACTION FACTOR

The Japanese have the intelligence to advance delight as one of their objectives of sound living. In our rage to be meager and solid, we frequently disregard one of the most fundamental blessings of presence—the joy and fulfillment that can be found in the eating experience. When you eat what you really need, in a welcoming and favorable situation, the joy you bring will be an incredible power to help you feel satisfied and satisfied.

By giving this experience to yourself, you will find that it takes significantly less food to choose you've had "enough."

1. Give yourself authorization to look for delight in your eating. The more pleasurable your food is, the more fulfillments you'll get from your eating experience. (The more fulfilled you feel, the less you'll have to eat—particularly on the off chance that you realize that this food will never be illegal.)

2. Make sense of what you truly need to eat by focusing on the accompanying sensations related with eating:

  a. Taste—sweet, appetizing, salty, acrid, or unpleasant

b. Surface—hard, crunchy, smooth, rich, and so forth.

c. Smell—sweet, harsh, gentle, and so forth.

d. Appearance—shading, shape, eye claim, and so forth.

e. Temperature—hot, cool, cold, calm

f. Volume or filling limit—vaporous, light, thick

3. Consider how your body may feel when you complete the process of eating:

a. Will you be physically fulfilled by your decision?

b. Will thick food make you feel awkwardly full later or a breezy food leaves you feeling unfilled?

c. Will an excessively rich supper give you stomach trouble?

d. Will an essentially sweet dinner send your glucose on an exciting ride?

4. Make your eating condition charming:

a. Eat when delicately hungry as opposed to eager for over.

b. Make time to value your food.

c. Create a stylish domain—attempt pretty placemats, candles, vivid dishes, traditional music. Keep the clamor level down.

d. Sit down to eat.

e. Take a few full breaths before you eat.

f. Savor your food.

g. Pay consideration regarding eating as gradually as possible.

h. Taste each nibble of food that you put in your mouth.

i. Provide assortment in your supper.

j. Avoid pressure while eating.

5. Try not to settle. Wipe out the unenjoyable—in the event that you don't cherish it, don't eat it, and on the off chance that you love it, relish it!

6. Check in with your taste buds amidst your dinner to check whether the food still tastes in the same class as it did when you started.

7. Keep in mind; it doesn't generally need to be great—a few times suppers are not in your control. There are a lot more open doors ahead for fulfilling suppers.

Stage 7-PRINCIPLE SEVEN: COPE WITH YOUR EMOTIONS WITHOUT USING FOOD

Discover approaches to comfort, sustain, divert, and resolve your issues without utilizing food. Nervousness, depression, weariness, and outrage are feelings we as a whole encounter all through life. Everyone has its very own trigger, and every ha its very own submission. Food won't fix any of these sentiments. It might comfort for the present moment, divert from the torment, or even numb you into a food headache; however food won't take care of the issue. In the event that anything, eating for an enthusiastic yearning will just exacerbate you feel over the long haul. You'll eventually need to manage the wellspring of the feeling, just as the distress of overeating.

1. Ask yourself: "Am I organically eager?" If your answer is truly, respect your appetite and eat!

2. When you end up looking for food however realize that you're not organically eager, take an opportunity to ask yourself, "What am I feeling?"

    a. Are you frightened, restless, furious, exhausted, harmed, desolate, discouraged? Or then again would you say you are upbeat, energized, need a prize, or need to celebrate?

    b. To help recognize your sentiments, invest some tranquil energy writing in your diary or talking into a recording device. Or on the other hand, if it's simpler to connect with your sentiments with someone else, call a decent companion or getting relative. You may even need to call your psychotherapist or food specialist. Use email if that is a simpler method to impart.

3. At that point ask yourself, "What do I need?"

    a. Do you really require a rest, an embrace, some intelligent incitement, and so on.? Food doesn't properly fulfill any of those requirements.

4. So as to get your needs met, ask: "Would you please?" Sometimes, for should be satisfied, you'll need to make some noise and request help.

5. Address your issues without utilizing food in the accompanying manners:

    a. Nurture yourself by washing up, tuning in to relieving music, getting a back rub, taking a yoga class, getting yourself a few blooms, and so on.

    b. Deal with your emotions. Recognize what is disturbing you. Enable your sentiments to develop. This will diminish your need to drive them down with food.

    c. If vital, give yourself an impermanent interruption. It's alright to escape from the sentiments now and again, yet you don't need to utilize food for this reason. Have a go at leasing a motion picture, perusing an engrossing book, tuning in to music or a book recording, cultivating, and so forth.

6. On the off chance that you have a scene of utilizing food to adapt, consider it to be a warning that something is going on in your life that requirements consideration. Whatever you do, don't pound yourself for this conduct. The vast majorities do it now and again—simply accept it as a learning encounter and go on.

Stage 8—PRINCIPLE EIGHT: RESPECT YOUR BODY

Acknowledge your hereditary outline. Similarly as an individual with a shoe size of eight would not hope to sensibly press into a size six, it is similarly as worthless (and awkward) to have a similar desire with body size. In any case, for the most part, regard your body, so you can rest easy thinking about who you are. It's difficult to dismiss the diet attitude in the event that you are unreasonable and excessively basic about your body shape.

1. Value the pieces of your body that you particularly like—regardless of whether it's your hair, midriff, feet, or nose.

2. Scrub down, and use salves and creams that vibe calming as you focus on them.

3. Get back rubs and embraces and strokes that offer your body the chance to be contacted.

4. Get settled. Purchase agreeable under-articles of clothing. Purchase apparel that is complimenting and fits you without being tight.

5. Try not to conceal your body in garments that are excessively huge.

6. Stop the body-check game. Quit contrasting yourself with every other person in the room. It blinds you from valuing yourself and is an arrangement for more body disappointment. It may even make a compulsion to come back to dieting.

7. Try not to bargain for the "Huge Event." Don't capitulate to the weight of "dieting down" to press into that uncommon outfit—it wills just blowback.

8. Stop body slamming. Each time you center on your defective body parts, it makes progressively hesitance and body stress. At the point when you hear yourself offering deriding remarks about your body, supplant these remarks with kind body proclamations.

9. Quit gauging yourself. It can just make you feel disappointed with your body.

10. Regard body decent variety, particularly yours.

11. Be reasonable about your hereditary cosmetics. Acknowledge your body type, and realize that your body is probably going to adjust at its regular weight when you're reliably tuning in to your intuitive signals and rehearsing self-care.

12. Be comprehension of yourself. Regard the way that you might be higher than your ordinary body weight on the off chance that you are somebody who has utilized food to adapt when you realized no other method to deal with your emotions, or in light of the fact that you've been a casualty of the diet attitude. Be delicate with yourself and acknowledge that your body is the place it is on the grounds that you had next to no decision about these variables.

Stage 9—PRINCIPLE NINE: EXERCISE—FEEL THE DIFFERENCE

Disregard aggressor work out. Simply get dynamic and feel the distinction. Shift your focus on how it feels to move your body, as opposed to the impact of calorie-consuming activity. On the off chance that you center on how you feel from turning out, for example, empowered, it can have the effect between turning up for an energetic morning walk and hitting the rest alarm. On the off chance that when you wake up, your solitary objective is to get more fit, it's typically not an inspiring element at that time of time.

1. Leap forward exercise obstructions:

a. Discover every one of the purposes for any activity obstruction that you may have. It might be expected to having been prodded as a kid, having re-belled against power, feeling threatened for not having a fit enough body, and so forth.

b. Focus on how it feels. Exercise is basically for feeling better. It so happens that the better you feel, the less you'll have to utilize food as an approach to adapt. It can likewise give you expanded vitality, a general atmosphere of prosperity, a feeling of strengthening, and sounder rest.

c. Disassociate practice from weight reduction. Delete the tape of how exercise felt when you were dieting. You presumably weren't getting enough calories or starches to give you the vitality to exercise and feel great simultaneously.

d. Focus on practice as a method for dealing with yourself, feeling great now and forestalling medical issues further down the road.

e. Don't get trapped in practice mind games, for example,

f. The, It's-Not-Worth It Trap—i.e., feeling it's not justified, despite any potential benefits in the event that it doesn't last a predetermined measure of time.

g. Couch-Potato Denial—being occupied isn't equivalent to physical action.

h. The No-Time-to-Spare Trap—figures out how to prioritize.

i. The If-I-Don't-Sweat-It-Doesn't-Count Trap—physical wellness doesn't need to mean thorough exercises.

2. Get dynamic in day by day living. Make practice helpful and fun:

a. Park your vehicle a couple of squares from your goal so you can add some strolling to your day.

b. Walk up stairs as opposed to utilizing the lift.

c. Ride your bicycle or stroll to work on the off chance that you live close enough.

d. When you travel, take strolling shoes or a bounce rope. Consider picking lodgings that have exercise offices.

3. Make practice fun.

   a. Consider playing a group activity, for example, volleyball (sea shore volleyball throughout the late spring), softball, ball, soccer, or tennis.

   b. Join an exercise center, if having others around you will propel you.

   c. Buy a treadmill or other home gym equipment and put a TV and DVR or DVD player before it so you can record and watch motion pictures or fascinating projects. Tuning in to music or a book recording may likewise make the activity progressively fun.

   d. Find an activity band together with whom you can go for strolls. Talking and strolling can make the walk progressively charming.

4. Make practice a nonnegotiable need.

5. Be agreeable while working out.

6. Incorporate quality preparing so you can remake muscle that was lost from dieting.

7. Incorporate extending as a feature of your activity schedule.

8. Remember rest. Ensure you give yourself long stretches of rest inside your activity week. It will forestall burnout, just as allowing your muscles to invigorate and fix.

Stage 10: TEN PRINCIPLE: HONOR YOUR HEALTH WITH SOFT NUTRITION

Decide on food decisions that respect your health and taste buds while making you feel good. Remember that it is not necessary to follow an ideal diet to be solid. Suddenly, you will not miss a supplement or get fat for a bite, a party or a day of food. It's what you eat reliably after some time that issues. Progress, not flawlessness, is what matters.

1. Think about the precepts of food insight: assortment, control, and equalization. Likewise with work out, think about food as your identification into feeling better.

2. Feed your digestion. Make certain to stir your metabolic fire by getting adequate fuel for the duration of the day by eating at whatever point you're eager.

3. Eat a lot of entire grains, leafy foods, and beans for their fiber content, so your stomach related tract functions

admirably. They're likewise a force place of nutrients, minerals, and phyto-synthetics.

4. Eat adequate protein, yet not all that much, for cell fix and creation of hormones, compounds, hair, nails, and so forth.

5. Eat a lot of starches and adequate calories so your protein can be utilized as a protein source and not be signed as a vitality source.

6. Take in a sufficient measure of dairy items to get enough calcium to keep your bones solid.

7. Drink a lot of water to help processing, forestall stoppage, have adequate blood volume, and wash down your kidneys.

8. Eat a sufficient measure of fat. We need fat in our diets consequently:

   a. to advance satiety,
   b. to help manufacture cell dividers, including synapses,
   c. for retention of fat solvent nutrients, and
   d. for creation of hormones.
   e. Whenever conceivable, pick quality fats, for example, avocado, olive oil, nuts, and so forth.

9. Take into account some play foods so as to offset your great health with joy and fulfillment. Leave the vast majority of your food decisions alone made for physical health, while some of them are for basic delight.

10. Try not to be tricked by the fat-free trip. Fat free doesn't mean calorie free or supplement thick. These foods will in general be restricted in supplements, while having an excess of sugar. Without fat foods frequently are not as fulfilling as low-fat foods. They likewise make a fantasy of being low-calorie and lead to overconsumption before you know it.

11. Get off the food pedestal. You don't need to be great. Respect your health, your taste buds, and your humanness.

EMOTIONAL

EATING

Break the Cycle, Say STOP Binge
Eating! A Proven 21-Day Program
Based on Ten Intuitive Principles for a
Healthy Relationship with Food. Be
Free from the Slavery of Hunger (Part
1)

By

Kelly Francis

content within this book has been derived from various sources. Please consult a licensed professional before attempting any techniques outlined in this book.

By reading this document, the reader agrees that under no circumstances is the author responsible for any losses, direct or indirect, which are incurred as a result of the use of information contained within this document, including, but not limited to, — errors, omissions, or inaccuracies.

INTRODUCTION

E motional Eating: Break the Cycle, Say STOP Binge Eating! A Proven-Effective 21-Day Program Based On Ten Intuitive Principles For A Healthy Relationship With Food. Find Freedom From Dieting Forever. Emotional eating is described as "the urge to eat in reaction to positive and negative feelings." While the word emotional eating mostly applies to eating as a means of coping with negative emotions, it also includes eating for positive emotions, such as eating food while enjoying an accomplishment or eating to boost an already good mood. Emotions often guide the feeding in these conditions but not in a negative way.

Any people get to terms with difficult situations by having comfort food. Chowing on ice cream or macaroni, and cheese will make it look like it's all right. And maybe there is an explanation why.

As points out, parts of the brain are punished with eating high-fat or high-sugar items. And more than a decade of psychological research shows that any rewarding activity would possibly replicate itself.

Emotional feeding means eating for purposes other than hunger. You can eat for being unhappy, upset, tired or lonely. Or you could be using food as a reward. Nutrition will find you relaxing and divert you from what really does concern you.

Eating comfort food as things get tough — also recognized as emotional eating or eating stress — is not, though, an answer to the challenges of life. It only works briefly. Worse, if it brings on weight gain, it creates longer-term anxiety.

Knowing what causes your emotional eating: Another way to control emotional eating is to find out what the symptoms are. Keep a food diary that not only tracks what you eat and how much but also how you felt at the time.

When you identify a trend, build a turnaround plan. For starters, if you often eat because you believe after a bad day you deserve it, realize that you also deserve to lose weight, feel healthy and be proud of yourself. If you are eating because of tension, learn to turn the discomfort down. Yoga, meditation and regular exercise may help to lower levels of stress.

Reasons of emotional eating: When finding out why you need comfort food you may be able to stop panic eating or emotional eating. Is it calming you down, cheering you up, making up for a bad day or a combination? Recognizing such patterns of thought can promote resistance to giving in. It also helps to understand that emotional eating is not solving the problem that led you to get angry.

The greatest breaks from emotional eating are activities that only require about five minutes switching gears— just long enough to help.

Several suggestions for moving strategies include: walking outside for a five-minute walk, turning on your favorite music and dancing, contacting a close friend to talk. The more ways you will think about entertaining yourself, the better it will become to stop eating tension over time. Instead it will become your new habit of fighting.

If you're an emotional eater, you may not notice the inherent signs of appetite and fullness in your body. You should eat more than you need or wish for.Emotional eating may interfere with making healthy choices regarding food. And it can keep you from getting to and remaining at a healthy weight.

What are symptoms of mental sustenance?

Everybody feeds from time to time, for purposes other than thirst. But if you find that out of hunger or for relaxation you sometimes search for food, you may be consuming for emotional reasons.

Common signs of emotional eating are: if you have more stress in your life, adjust your eating habits.
Feed if you're not thirsty, or are full.
Eating to soothe feelings.
Meat is used as a compliment.
Eating so as not to contend with a stressful situation.

Identify the emotional eating symptoms
One way to find out what emotional eating causes is to keep a diary of food. Factor in when and what you're doing. Write down also what you do and felt before you started eating. To find patterns in your eating habits, you can use this knowledge. For starters, you might find that you purchase an unhealthy snack from the office vending machine any time you start thinking about an assignment at work.

Use a scale of hunger: A scale of hunger will help you learn how to tell the difference between real, actual hunger and hunger in your mind. Psychological appetite is an eating impulse triggered by feelings, such as pain, anxiety, disappointment, or joy.

Value your appetite on a scale of 1 to 10 as you start feeling like you want something to eat, with 1 starving and 10 being so loaded you feel sick. A 5 or 6 rating means that you're comfortable— neither too hungry nor too whole.

Emotional eating is a form of reducing or relaxing negative emotions, such as tension, rage, anxiety, depression, sorrow and loneliness. Major events in life or, more generally, the daily life hassles may cause negative emotions that contribute to emotional eating and hinder the attempts to lose weight.

1—Starving, exhausted, dizzy 2—Very thin, cranky, low-energy, plenty of stomach rumbling 3—Pretty tired, stomach rumbling a little 4—Starting to feel a little better 5—Satisfied, neither hungry nor complete 6—A little full, comfortably full 7—A little awkward 8—Feeling bloated 9—Very cramped, stomach hurts 10—So loaded you feel sick

Use the scale to evaluate your appetite. If you feel like eating but your degree of hunger is a scale 6 or higher, pause and test your emotions.

Unpleasant eating happens when the diet becomes the reaction of an individual to certain unpleasant internal or external signals. The emotional eater may consume comfort foods rather than dealing in their thoughts and the stress they put in in an effort to distract themselves from the pain. This also includes, in most situations, a form of compulsive overeating that results in an overly full stomach sensation. Of reality, consuming this sort of food does not come without negative side effects. Three of the most famous are in the order.

Weight-related health concerns: Depression, high blood pressure, exhaustion and high cholesterol are all health issues that may come from frequent emotional eating outbursts.

Guilt: They're usually filled with guilt and shame for what they've done after the emotional "threat" has passed and the emotional overeater has eaten up. This guilt may contribute to another episode of emotional eating or low self-esteem.

Diarrhea: As nervous eaters often over-eat or eat too fast and suffer stomach pain or diarrhea afterwards, because the sight of food in the stomach acts as a diversion to the feelings they are trying to avoid. It can last a day or two after the actual meal.

We don't forever eat simply to satisfy physical hunger. several folks conjointly communicate food for comfort, stress relief, or to reward ourselves. And after we do, we tend to tend to succeed in for food, sweets, and different comforting however unhealthy foods. you may reach for a pint of frozen dessert once you're feeling down, order a pizza pie if you're bored or lonely, or swing by the drive-through once a nerve-wracking day at work. Emotional feeding is exploitation food to form yourself feel better—to fill emotional desires, instead of your abdomen. sadly, emotional feeding doesn't fix emotional issues. In fact, it always causes you to feel worse. Afterward, not solely will the first emotional issue stay, however you furthermore mght feel guilty for mortal sin.

People who showing emotion eat reach for food many times every week or a lot of to suppress and soothe negative feelings. they will even feel guilt or shame once feeding this manner, resulting in a cycle of excess feeding and associated problems, like weight gain.

The emotional feeding cycle
Occasionally exploitation food as a pick-me-up, a reward, or to celebrate isn't essentially a nasty factor. however once feeding is your primary emotional header mechanism— when your 1st impulse is to open the white goods whenever you're stressed, upset, angry, lonely, exhausted, or bored— you grind to a halt in an unhealthy cycle wherever the important feeling or drawback is rarely addressed .

Emotional hunger can't be crammed with food. feeding could feel sensible within the moment, however the sentiments that triggered the feeding are still there. And you regularly feel worse than you probably did before owing to the uncalled-for calories you've simply consumed. You beat yourself for messing up and not having a lot of resolution.

Compounding the matter, you stop learning healthier ways in which to upset your emotions, you've got a more durable and harder time dominant your weight, and you are feeling more and more overcome over each food and your feelings. however in spite of however overcome you are feeling over food and your feelings, it's potential to form a positive amendment. you'll be able to learn healthier ways in which to upset your emotions, avoid triggers, conquer cravings, and at last place a stop to emotional feeding.

The distinction between emotional hunger and physical hunger

Before you'll be able to become independent from from the cycle of emotional feeding, you initially got to learn the way to differentiate between emotional and physical hunger. this will be trickier than it sounds, particularly if you frequently use food to upset your feelings.

Emotional hunger will be powerful, thus it's simple to mistake it for physical hunger. however there are clues you'll be able to seek for to assist you tell physical and emotional hunger apart.

Emotional hunger comes on suddenly. It hits you in an immediate and feels overwhelming and pressing. Physical hunger, on the opposite hand, comes on a lot of bit by bit.

The urge to eat doesn't feel as dire or demand instant satisfaction (unless you haven't ingested for a awfully long time).

Emotional hunger craves specific comfort foods. once you're physically hungry, nearly something sounds good—including healthy stuff like vegetables. however emotional hunger craves food or sugar-coated snacks that offer an immediate rush. you are feeling such as you would like cheesecake or pizza pie, and zilch else can do.

Emotional hunger usually results in mindless feeding. Before you recognize it, you've ingested an entire bag of chips or an entire pint of frozen dessert while not extremely listening or totally enjoying it. once you're feeding in response to physical hunger, you're usually a lot of awake to what you're doing.

Emotional hunger isn't glad once you're full. you retain wanting a lot of and more, usually feeding till you're uncomfortably stuffed. Physical hunger, on the opposite hand, doesn't got to be stuffed. you are feeling glad once your abdomen is full.

Emotional hunger isn't set within the abdomen. instead of a growling belly or a pang in your abdomen, you are feeling your hunger as a desire you can't get out of your head. You're targeted on specific textures, tastes, and smells.

Emotional hunger usually results in regret, guilt, or shame. after you eat to satisfy physical hunger, you're unlikely to feel guilty or mortified as a result of you're merely giving your body what it desires. If you are feeling guilty once you eat, it's probably as a result of you recognize at bottom that you're not feeding for organic process reasons.

Emotional hunger vs. Physical hunger

Emotional hunger comes on suddenly Physical hunger comes on bit by bit

Emotional hunger looks like it must be glad instantly Physical hunger will wait

Emotional hunger craves specific comfort foods Physical hunger is receptive options—lots of things sound sensible

Emotional hunger isn't glad with a full abdomen. Physical hunger stops once you're full

Emotional feeding triggers feelings of guilt, quality, and shame feeding to satisfy physical hunger doesn't cause you to feel dangerous regarding yourself

Identify your emotional feeding triggers

The first step in putt a stop to emotional feeding is distinctive your personal triggers. What things, places, or feelings cause you to reach for the comfort of food? Most emotional feeding is coupled to unpleasant feelings, however it may be triggered by positive emotions, like appreciated yourself for achieving a goal or celebrating a vacation or blessed event.

CHAPTER 1:

Common causes of emotional feeding

Stress – Ever notice however stress causes you to hungry? It's not simply in your mind. once stress is chronic, because it thus usually is in our chaotic, fast world, your body produces high levels of the strain secretion, cortisol. corticoid triggers cravings for salty, sweet, and deep-fried foods—foods that provide you with a burst of energy and pleasure. The a lot of uncontrolled stress in your life, the a lot of probably you're to show to food for emotional relief.

Stuffing emotions – feeding will be the way to briefly silence or "stuff down" uncomfortable emotions, as well as anger, fear, sadness, anxiety, loneliness, resentment, and shame. whereas you're desensitising yourself with food, you'll be able to avoid the tough emotions you'd rather not feel.

Boredom or feelings of emptiness – does one ever eat merely to offer yourself one thing to try to to, to alleviate tedium, or as the way to fill a void in your life? you are feeling unrealized and empty, and food could be a thanks to occupy your mouth and it slow. within the moment, it fills you up and distracts you from underlying feelings of aimlessness and discontentment together with your life.

Childhood habits – remember to your childhood recollections of food. Did your oldsters reward sensible behavior with frozen dessert, take you out for pizza pie after you got an honest information, or serve you sweets after you were feeling sad? These habits will usually carry over into adulthood. Or your feeding is also driven by nostalgia—for cherished recollections of cooking burgers within the curtilage together with your pappa or baking and eating cookies with your female parent.

Social influences – obtaining along with others for a meal could be a good way to alleviate stress, however it may cause mortal sin. It's simple to satiate just because the food is there or because everybody else is feeding. you will conjointly satiate in social things out of nervousness. Or maybe your family or circle of friends encourages you to satiate, and it's easier to travel in conjunction with the cluster.

Keep an emotional feeding diary

You probably recognized yourself in a minimum of some of the previous descriptions. however nevertheless, you'll wish to urge even a lot of specific. one in all the simplest ways in which to spot the patterns behind your emotional feeding is to stay track with a food and mood diary.

Every time you satiate or feel compelled to succeed in for your version of food Kryptonite, take an instant to work out what triggered the urge. If you turn back, you'll typically realize associate displeasing event that kicked of the emotional feeding cycle. Write it all down in your food and mood diary: what you Greek deity (or wished to eat), what happened to upset you, however you felt before you Greek deity, what you felt as you were feeding, and the way you felt later on.

Over time, you'll see a pattern emerge. perhaps you usually find yourself gorging yourself once outlay time with a essential friend. Or maybe you stress eat whenever you're on a point or after you attend family functions. Once you determine your emotional feeding triggers, succeeding step is distinctive healthier ways in which to feed your feelings.

Find different ways in which to feed your feelings

If you don't shrewdness to manage your emotions in a very manner that doesn't involve food, you won't be able to management your feeding habits for terribly long. Diets thus usually fail as a result of they provide logical organic process recommendation that solely works if you've got aware management over your feeding habits. It doesn't work once emotions hijack the method, exigent an instantaneous payoff with food.

In order to prevent emotional feeding, you've got to search out different ways in which to satisfy yourself showing emotion. It's not enough to know the cycle of emotional feeding or perhaps to understand your triggers, though that's an enormous opening move. you would like alternatives to food that you just will communicate for emotional fulfillment.

CHAPTER 2:

Alternatives to emotional feeding

I f you're depressed or lonely, decision somebody who forever causes you to feel higher, play together with your dog or cat, or check up on a favourite pic or cherished souvenir.

If you're anxious, expend your nervous energy by performing arts to your favorite song, compressing a stress ball, or taking a brisk walk.

If you're exhausted, treat yourself with a hot cup of tea, take a shower, lightweight some scented candles, or wrap yourself in a very heat blanket.

If you're bored, scan an honest book, watch a comedy show, explore the outside, or communicate associate activity you get pleasure from (woodworking, taking part in the stringed instrument, shooting hoops, scrapbooking, etc.).

Pause once cravings hit and sign on with yourself

Most emotional eaters feel overcome over their food cravings. once the urge to eat hits, it's all you'll be able to have confidence. you are feeling associate nearly unendurable tension that demands to be fed, right now! as a result of you've tried to resist within the past and unsuccessful, you think that your resolution simply isn't up to snuff. however the reality is that you just have a lot of power over your cravings than you're thinking that.

Take five before you throw in the towel to a desire

Emotional feeding tends to be automatic and nearly mindless. Before you even understand what you're doing, you've reached for a bath of frozen dessert and polished off 1/2 it. however if you'll be able to take an instant to pause and mirror once you're hit with a desire, you offer yourself the chance to form a distinct call.

Can you suspend feeding for 5 minutes? or simply begin with one minute. Don't tell yourself you can't throw in the towel to the craving; bear in mind, the taboo is very tempting. simply tell yourself to attend.

While you're waiting, sign on with yourself. however are you feeling? What's occurring emotionally? albeit you finish up feeding, you'll have an improved understanding of why you probably did it. this will assist you set yourself up for a distinct response next time.

Learn to simply accept your feelings—even the dangerous ones

While it should appear that the core drawback is that you're overcome over food, emotional feeding really stems from feeling overcome over your emotions. You don't feel capable of addressing your feelings head on, thus you avoid them with food.

Allowing yourself to feel uncomfortable emotions will be chilling. you will concern that, like Pandora's box, once you open the door you won't be able to shut it. however the reality is that after we don't obsess over or suppress our emotions, even the foremost painful and tough feelings subside comparatively quickly and lose their power to manage our attention.

To do this you would like to become conscious and learn the way to remain connected to your moment-to-moment emotional expertise. this will modify you to rein in stress and repair emotional issues that always trigger emotional feeding. HelpGuide's free Emotional Intelligence Toolkit will show you ways.

Indulge while not mortal sin by degustation your food

When you eat to feed your feelings, you tend to try to to thus quickly, senselessly intense food on autopilot. You eat thus quick you miss out on the various tastes and textures of your food—as well as your body's cues that you're full and not hungry. however by retardation down and degustation each bite, you'll not solely get pleasure from your food a lot of however you'll even be less probably to satiate.

Slowing down and degustation your food is a very important facet of conscious eating, the alternative of mindless, emotional feeding. attempt taking some deep breaths before beginning your food, putt your utensils down between bites, and extremely specializing in the expertise of feeding. listen to the textures, shapes, colours and smells of your food. however will every mouthful taste? however does it create your body feel? By retardation down during this manner, you'll realize you appreciate every bite of food way more. you'll be able to even fancy your favorite foods and feel full on a lot of less. It takes time for the body's fullness signal to succeed in your brain, thus taking some moments to contemplate however you are feeling once every bite—hungry or satiated—can assist you avoid mortal sin.

Practice conscious feeding

Eating whereas you're conjointly doing different things—such as looking TV, driving, or fidgeting with your phone—can forestall you from totally enjoying your food. Since your mind is elsewhere, you will not feel glad or continue feeding even supposing you're not hungry. feeding a lot of heedfully will facilitate focus your mind on your food and therefore the pleasure of a meal and curb mortal sin. See conscious feeding.

Support yourself with healthy life-style habits

When you're physically robust, relaxed, and well reinvigorated, you're higher able to handle the curveballs that life inevitably throws your manner. however once you're already exhausted and flooded, any very little hiccup has the potential to send you off the rails and straight toward the white goods. Exercise, sleep, and different healthy life-style habits can assist you get through tough times while not emotional feeding.

Make daily exercise a priority. Physical activity will wonders for your mood and energy levels, and it's conjointly a robust stress reducer. And moving into the exercise habit sophisticated} than you will assume.

Aim for eight hours of sleep nightly. after you don't get the sleep you would like, your body craves sugar-coated foods that may provide you with a fast energy boost. obtaining lots of rest can facilitate with appetency management and scale back food cravings.

Make time for relaxation.Give yourself permission to require a minimum of half-hour a day to relax, decompress, and unwind. this is often it slow to require a prospect from your responsibilities and recharge your batteries.

Connect with others. Don't underestimate the importance of shut relationships and social activities. outlay time with positive those who enhance your life can facilitate defend you from the negative effects of stress.

What causes somebody to eat owing to their emotions? Anything from work stress to money worries, health problems to relationship struggles is also the basis cause of your emotional feeding.

It's a problem that affects each sexes. however in keeping with completely different studies, emotional feeding is a lot of common with ladies than with men.

Why food?

Negative emotions could cause a sense of emptiness or associate emotional void. Food is believed to be the way to fill that void and make a false feeling of "fullness" or temporary wholeness.

Other factors include:

retreating from social support throughout times of emotional would like not partaking in activities which may otherwise relieve stress, sadness, and so on not understanding the distinction between physical and emotional hunger using negative self-talking that's associated with bingeing episodes. this will produce a cycle of emotional feeding changing corticoid levels in response to worry, resulting in cravings.

Emotional feeding affects each men and girls. it should be caused by variety of things, as well as stress, secretion changes, or mixed hunger cues.

Physical hunger vs Emotional hunger

It develops slowly over time. It comes regarding suddenly or suddenly.

You need a spread of food teams. You crave solely bound foods.

You feel the feeling of fullness and take it as a cue to prevent feeding. you will binge on food and not feel a sensation of fullness.

You have no negative feelings regarding feeding. you are feeling guilt or shame regarding feeding.

Physical and emotional hunger is also simply confused, however there are key variations between the 2. listen to however and once your hunger starts similarly as how you are feeling once feeding.

How to stop emotional feeding

Emotional hunger isn't simply squelched by feeding

While filling up may fit within the moment, feeding owing to negative emotions usually leaves folks feeling a lot of upset than before. This cycle usually doesn't finish till someone addresses emotional desires head on.

Find different ways in which to deal with stress

Discovering otherwise to upset negative emotions is usually the primary step toward overcoming emotional feeding. this might mean writing in a very journal, reading a book, or finding some minutes to otherwise relax and decompress from the day.

It takes time to shift your outlook from reaching for food to partaking in different styles of stress relief, thus experiment with a spread of activities to search out what works for you.

Move your body

Some folks realize relief in obtaining regular exercise. A walk or jog round the block or a fix yoga routine could facilitate in notably emotional moments.

In one study, participants were asked to have interaction in eight weeks of yoga. They were then assessed on their attentiveness and perceptive understanding — essentially their understanding of themselves and of things close them.

The results showed that regular yoga is also a helpful preventative live to assist diffuse emotional states like anxiety and depression.

Try meditation

Others are calmed by turning inward to practices like meditation.

There are a spread of studies that support attentiveness meditation as a treatment for binge upset and emotional feeding.

Simple deep respiratory is meditation that you just will do nearly anyplace. Sit in a very quiet house and target your breath — slowly flowing in and out of your nostrils.

You can browse sites like YouTube for free of charge target-hunting meditations. for instance, mythical being Stephenson's "Guided Meditation for Anxiety & Stress" has over four million views and goes through a series of visual image and respiratory exercises for over half-hour.

Start a food diary

Keeping a log of what you eat and after you eat it should assist you determine triggers that cause emotional feeding. you'll be able to jot notes in a very notebook or communicate technology with an app like MyFitnessPal.

While it will be difficult, try and embrace everything you eat — but huge or little — and record the emotions you're feeling in this moment.

Also, if you decide on to hunt medical facilitate regarding your feeding habits, your food diary will be a great tool to share together with your doctor.

Eat a healthy diet

Making sure you get enough nutrients to fuel your body is additionally key. It will be tough to differentiate between true and emotional hunger. If you eat well throughout the day, it should be easier to identify once you're feeding out of tedium or unhappiness or stress.

Still having trouble? attempt reaching for healthy snacks, like contemporary fruit or vegetables, plain popcorn, and different low-fat, low-calorie foods.

Take common things out of your storage room

Consider trashing or donating foods in your cabinets that you just usually reach for in moments of strife. assume high-fat, sweet or calorie-laden things, like chips, chocolate, and frozen dessert. conjointly table journeys to the market once you're feeling upset.

Keeping the foods you crave out of reach once you're feeling emotional could facilitate break the cycle by supplying you with time to assume before noshing.

Pay attention to volume

Resist grabbing an entire bag of chips or different food to snack on. activity out parts and selecting little plates to assist with portion management are conscious feeding habits to figure on developing.

Once you've finished one serving to, offer yourself time before going back for a second. you will even wish to undertake another stress-relieving technique, like deep respiratory, within the meanwhile.

Seek support

Resist isolation in moments of unhappiness or anxiety. Even a fast telephone call to an acquaintance or loved one will do wonders for your mood. There are formal support teams which will facilitate.

Overeaters Anonymous is a corporation that addresses mortal sin from emotional eating, compulsive overeating, and different feeding disorders.

Your doctor could provide you with a referral to a counselor or coach who will assist you determine the emotions at the route of your hunger. realize different teams in your space by looking out on social sites like Meetup.

Banish distractions
You may end up feeding ahead of the tv, computer, or another distraction. attempt change off the tube or putt down your phone succeeding time you discover yourself during this pattern.

By specializing in your food, the bites you're taking, and your level of hunger, you will discover that you're feeding showing emotion. Some even realize it useful to target manduction ten to thirty times before swallowing a bite of food.

CHAPTER 3:

Doing this stuff provides your mind time to catch up to your abdomen.

Work on positive self-talk

Feelings of shame and guilt are related to emotional feeding. It's necessary to figure on the self-talk you expertise once associate episode — or it should cause a cycle of emotional feeding behavior.

Instead of coming back down onerous, attempt learning from your black eye. Use it as a chance to arrange for the long run. And make certain to reward yourself with self-care measures — taking a shower, going for a leisurely walk, then on — after you create strides.

Food could facilitate ease emotions ab initio, however addressing the sentiments behind the hunger is vital within the future. Work to search out other ways to upset stress, like exercise and peer support, and check out active conscious feeding habits.

When to examine your doctor
It's diligence, however attempt gazing your emotional feeding as a chance to urge a lot of connected with yourself and your feelings.

Taking the method day by day can eventually cause an improved understanding of yourself, similarly as toward the event of more healthy feeding habits.

Left unaddressed, emotional feeding could cause binge upset or different eating disorders.

It's necessary to examine your doctor if you are feeling you're feeding patterns are out of your management. Your doctor could refer you to a counselor or dietician to assist address each the mental and physical facet of emotional feeding.

Sometimes the strongest food cravings hit once you're at your weakest purpose showing emotion. you will communicate food for comfort — consciously or unconsciously — once facing a tough drawback, feeling stressed or perhaps feeling bored.

Emotional feeding will sabotage your weight-loss efforts. It usually results in feeding an excessive amount of — particularly too much of high-calorie, sweet and fatty foods. the great news is that if you're susceptible to emotional feeding, you'll be able to take steps to regain management of your feeding habits and find back on course together with your weight-loss goals.

How the food-weight loss cycle works
Emotional feeding is eating as the way to suppress or soothe negative emotions, like stress, anger, fear, boredom, unhappiness and loneliness. Major life events or, a lot of unremarkably, the hassles of existence will trigger negative emotions that cause emotional feeding and disrupt your weight-loss efforts. These triggers would possibly include:
Relationship conflicts
Fatigue
Financial pressures
Health issues
Work or different stressors

Although some folks eat less within the face of robust emotions, if you're in emotional distress you may communicate impulsive or binge feeding, quickly intense whatever's convenient while not enjoyment.

In fact, your emotions will become thus tied to your feeding habits that you just mechanically reach for a treat whenever you're angry or stressed stupidly regarding what you're doing.

Food conjointly is a distraction. If you're troubled regarding a future event or stewing over a conflict, as an example, you will target feeding food rather than addressing the painful state of affairs.

Whatever emotions drive you to eat, the tip result's usually identical. The result is temporary, the emotions come and you probably then bear the extra burden of guilt regarding setting back your weight-loss goal. this will conjointly cause an unhealthy cycle — your emotions trigger you to satiate, you beat yourself up for obtaining off your weight-loss track, you are feeling dangerous and you satiate once more.

Most people assume emotional feeding is because of a scarcity of self-control. However, in my intensive work with feeding disorders and disordered eating, i might say that's seldom the case. If emotional feeding were a straightforward issue of discipline, we tend to might simply realize this discipline while not torturing ourselves over meal plans, paying cash for special diets, and perpetually obsessing regarding who is feeding what and once. And, of course, there would be no feeding disorders.

CHAPTER 4:

How does one go back to on track?

W hen negative emotions threaten to trigger emotional feeding, you'll be able to take steps to manage cravings. to assist stop emotional feeding, attempt these tips:

Keep a food diary. Write down what you eat, what proportion you eat, after you eat, how you're feeling after you eat and the way hungry you're. Over time, you may see patterns that reveal the association between mood and food. Tame your stress. If stress contributes to your emotional feeding, attempt a stress management technique, like yoga, meditation or deep respiratory.

Have a hunger reality check. Is your hunger physical or emotional? If you Greek deity simply some hours agone and don't have a rumbling abdomen, you're in all probability not hungry. offer the desire time to pass.

Get support. You're a lot of probably to offer in to emotional feeding if you lack an honest support network. contact family and friends or contemplate connection a support cluster.

Fight tedium. rather than snacking once you're not hungry, distract yourself and substitute a healthier behavior. Take a walk, watch a motion picture, play together with your cat, hear music, read, surf the net or decision an acquaintance.

Take away temptation. Don't keep hard-to-resist comfort foods in your home. And if you are feeling angry or blue, table your trip to the market till you've got your emotions in restraint.

Don't deprive yourself. once making an attempt to reduce, you may limit calories an excessive amount of, eat identical foods repeatedly and banish treats. this might simply serve to extend your food cravings, particularly in response to emotions. Eat satisfying amounts of healthier foods, get pleasure from associate occasional treat and find lots of selection to assist curb cravings.

Snack healthy. If you are feeling the urge to eat between meals, select a healthy snack, like contemporary fruit, vegetables with low-fat dip, kooky or unbuttered popcorn.

Or attempt lower calorie versions of your favorite foods to examine if they satisfy your desire.

Learn from setbacks. If you've got associate episode of emotional feeding, forgive yourself and begin contemporary succeeding day. try and learn from the expertise and create a concept for the way you'll be able to forestall it within the future. target the positive changes you're making in your feeding habits and provides yourself credit for creating changes that'll cause higher health.

What I even have to mention on this subject material isn't original; but, generally a repeating of the knowledge will function a useful reminder. Over and another time, I see the subsequent 5 factors that contribute to emotional feeding.

1. unknowingness

Emotional feeding will be a right away results of not being attentive to what or why you're eating. Therapists decision this unconscious feeding. Unconscious feeding is once you're through with your meal, and you still decide at it, slowly feeding the remaining portion that you just meant to depart behind. It may be putt peanuts or fruity or the other food in your mouth, simply because it's ahead of you.

The solution? try and stay conscious of what and after you are feeding. i do know it will be tedious to focus utterly on your feeding, particularly at first! begin slowly and avoid self-judgment as you are attempting out a replacement manner of being.

2. Food As Your solely Pleasure

I've usually asked folks what they might got to feel if they didn't binge or satiate, and therefore the common answer is, "I would don't have anything to seem forward to." And at the tip of an extended and agitated day, an enormous bowl of frozen dessert will be particularly effective in briefly soothing our exhausted, hard-working selves. Why? in keeping with several sources (e.g. this article), feeding sugars and fats releases opioids in our brains. Opioids are the active ingredients in cocain, heroin, and lots of different narcotics. that the calming, soothing effects you are feeling after you eat frozen dessert and BBQ potato chips are real. And breaking these habits will be like kicking a drug habit.

The solution? realize different ways in which to reward and soothe yourself besides food (and other dangerous behaviors). can these different ways in which be as effective at soothing you as food? fully not! the items you return up with will facilitate somewhat, however so as to actually surrender emotional feeding, you're conjointly aiming to got to apply tolerating tough feelings.

3. Inability to Tolerate tough Feelings

In our culture, we tend to learn from a young age to avoid things that feel dangerous. sadly, the ways in which we've found to distract ourselves from tough feelings aren't forever in our greatest interests. while not the power to tolerate experiencing life's inevitable foul feelings, you're liable to emotional feeding.

The solution? apply lease yourself expertise tough feelings. I know, a lot of easier aforementioned than done! i do know you don't like feeling mad, sad, rejected, and bored. and folks usually solicit from me, "What's the purpose in feeling mad? It doesn't amendment something." Well, it should not amendment the supply of your anger, however it'll forestall you from having to blunt your feelings with behaviors you'd prefer to stop — like feeding.

4. Body Hate

It may sound unreasonable, however it's true: Hating your body is one in all the largest factors in emotional feeding. Negativity, shame, and emotion seldom inspire folks to form long-lived nice changes, particularly once it involves our bodies or our sense of self. many of us tell ME they're going to stop hating their body once they reach their goal weight. I say you've got to prevent hating your body before you'll be able to stop the emotional feeding cycle.

The solution? sadly, this one is multi-layered, complicated, and distinctive for every person. to actually create permanent progress during this space needs over what's potential on behalf of me talk about in a very diary post. Sorry, friends!

5. Physiology

Letting yourself get too hungry or too tired is that the best thanks to leave yourself at risk of emotional feeding. once your body is hungry or tired, it not solely sends robust messages to your brain that signal it to eat, however once we're hungry and tired, we're not on our A game. This leaves us less equipped to defend cravings or urges.

The solution? You guessed it! Get lots of sleep, and eat many little meals throughout the day. (I'm a genius, right?) i do know you're aiming to tell ME that you just don't have time, however if your goal is to prevent emotional feeding, you're aiming to got to create those 2 things a priority. there's no manner around it.

Emotional feeding could be a powerful and effective thanks to realize temporary relief from several of life's challenges. If it didn't work thus well, nobody would get it on. so as to prevent this cycle of emotional feeding, you've got to form a commitment to succeed in deep within yourself to search out an area of grit and strength, and hopefully the higher than reminders will assist you in your journey.

Characteristics of emotional eating

Emotional feeding typically happens once one is trying to satisfy his or her epicurean drive, or the drive to eat palatable food to get pleasure within the absence of an energy deficit however may occur once one is seeking food as a bequest, feeding for social reasons (such as eating at a party), or feeding to evolve (which involves eating as a result of friends or family desires the individual to). once one is partaking in emotional feeding, they're typically seeking out palatable foods (such as sweets) instead of simply food normally. In some cases, emotional feeding can cause one thing referred to as "mindless eating" throughout that the individual is eating while not being conscious of what or what proportion they're consuming; this will occur during each positive and negative settings.

Emotional hunger doesn't originate from the abdomen, like with a rumbling or growling abdomen, however tends to begin once someone is concerned a desire or desires one thing specific to eat. Emotional responses are completely different. Giving in to a desire or feeding owing to stress will cause feelings of regret, shame, or guilt, and these responses tend to be related to emotional hunger. On the opposite hand, satisfying a physical hunger is giving the body the nutrients or calories it must perform and isn't related to negative feelings.

Major theories behind feeding

Current analysis suggests that bound individual factors could increase one's chance of exploitation emotional feeding as a header strategy. The inadequate have an effect on regulation theory posits that people interact in emotional feeding as a result of they believe mortal sin alleviates negative feelings. Escape theory builds upon inadequate have an effect on regulation theory by suggesting that folks not solely satiate to deal with negative emotions, however they realize that mortal sin diverts their attention off from a stimuli that's threatening shallowness to target a pleasant stimuli like food.

Restraint theory suggests that mortal sin as a results of negative emotions happens among people who already restrain their eating. whereas these people usually limit what they eat, once they are round-faced with negative emotions they cope by partaking in emotional feeding. Restraint theory supports the thought that people with different feeding disorders are a lot of probably to have interaction in emotional eating. along these 3 theories counsel that associate individual's aversion to negative emotions, notably negative feelings that arise in response to a threat to the ego or intense awareness, increase the propensity for the individual to utilize emotional feeding as a way of handling this aversion.

The biological stress response may additionally contribute to the event of emotional feeding tendencies. in a very crisis, corticotropin-releasing secretion (CRH) is secreted by the neural structure, suppressing appetency and triggering the discharge of glucocorticoids from the endocrine. These steroid hormones increase appetency and, unlike CRH, stay within the blood for a chronic amount of your time, usually leading to hyperphagia. those that expertise this biologically instigated increase in appetency throughout times of stress are thus fit to have confidence emotional feeding as a header mechanism.

CHAPTER 5:

Contributing factors

Negative effect

Overall, high levels of the negative have an effect on attribute are associated with emotional feeding. Negative affectivity could be a temperament attribute involving negative emotions and poor self-concept. Negative emotions old among negative have an effect on embrace anger, guilt, and nervousness. it's been found that bound negative have an effect on regulation scales expected emotional feeding.

An inability to articulate and determine one's emotions created the individual feel inadequate at regulation negative have an effect on and so a lot of probably to have interaction in emotional feeding as a way for handling those negative emotions. additional scientific studies concerning the link between negative have an effect on and feeding realize that, once experiencing a nerve-wracking event, food consumption is related to reduced feelings of negative have an effect on (i.e. feeling less bad) for those enduring high levels of chronic stress. This relationship between feeding and feeling higher suggests a self-reinforcing alternate pattern between high levels of chronic stress and consumption of extremely palatable foods as a header mechanism. Contrarily, a study conducted. found that negative have an effect on isn't considerably associated with emotional feeding, however the 2 are indirectly associated through emotion-focused header and avoidance-distraction behaviors. whereas the scientific results differed somewhat, they each counsel that negative have an effect on will play a job in emotional feeding however it should be accounted for by different variables.

Childhood development

For some folks, emotional feeding could be a learned behavior. throughout childhood, their oldsters offer them treats to assist them upset a troublesome day or state of affairs, or as a bequest for one thing sensible. Over time, the kid who reaches for a cookie once obtaining a nasty grade on a take a look at could become associate adult who grabs a box of cookies after a rough day at work. In associate example like this, the roots of emotional feeding are deep, which may create breaking the habit very difficult. In some cases, people could eat order to conform; for instance, people is also told "you got to end your plate" and therefore the individual could eat past the purpose during which they feel glad.

Related disorders

Emotional feeding as a way to cope is also a precursor to developing eating disorders like binge eating or bulimia nervosa. the link between emotional feeding and different disorders is basically because of the very fact that emotional eating and these disorders share key characteristics. a lot of specifically, they're each associated with feeling targeted header, maladjustive header ways, and a robust aversion to negative feelings and stimuli. it's necessary to notice that the causative direction has not been definitively established, that means that whereas emotional feeding is taken into account a precursor to those eating disorders, it conjointly is also the consequence of those disorders. The latter hypothesis that emotional feeding happens in response to a different upset is supported by analysis that has shown emotional eating to be a lot of common among people already tormented by bulimia nervosa.

Biological and environmental factors

Stress affects food preferences. various studies — granted, several of them in animals — have shown that physical or emotional distress will increase the intake of food high in fat, sugar, or both, even within the absence of caloric deficits.Once eaten, fat- and sugar-filled foods appear to possess a feedback result that dampens stress connected responses and emotions, as these foods trigger Intropin and opioid releases, that defend against the negative consequences of stress. These foods extremely are "comfort" foods in this they appear to counteract stress, however rat studies demonstrate that intermittent access to and consumption of those extremely palatable foods creates symptoms that jibe opioid withdrawal, suggesting that high -fat and high-sugar foods will become neurologically habit-forming some examples from the yank diet would include: hamburgers, pizza, french-fried potatoes, sausages and savory pasties. the foremost common food preferences are in decreasing order from: sweet energy-dense food, non-sweet energy-dense food then, fruits and vegetables. This might contribute to people's stress-induced looking for those foods.

The stress response could be a highly-individualized reaction and private variations in physiological reactivity may additionally contribute to the event of emotional feeding habits. ladies are a lot of probably than men to resort to feeding as a header mechanism for stress, as are fat people and people with histories of dietary restraint. In one study, ladies were exposed to associate hour-long social agent task or a neutral control. the ladies were exposed to every condition on completely different days. once the tasks, the ladies were invited to a buffet with each healthy and unhealthy snacks. those that had high chronic stress levels and a coffee corticoid reactivity to the acute stress task consumed considerably a lot of calories from cake than ladies with low chronic stress levels once each management and stress conditions. High corticoid levels, together with high hypoglycaemic agent levels, is also accountable for stress-induced feeding, as analysis shows high corticoid reactivity is related to hyperphagia, associate abnormally raised appetency for food, throughout stress.what is more, since glucocorticoids trigger hunger and specifically increase one's appetency for high-fat and high-sugar foods, those whose adrenal glands naturally secrete larger quantities of glucocorticoids in response to a agent are a lot of inclined toward hyperphagia. in addition, those whose bodies need longer to clear the blood of excess glucocorticoids are equally susceptible.

These biological factors will move with environmental components to additional trigger hyperphagia. Frequent intermittent stressors trigger continual, isolated releases of glucocorticoids in intervals too short to permit for a whole come to baseline levels, resulting in sustained and elevated levels of appetency. Therefore, those whose lifestyles or careers entail frequent intermittent stressors over prolonged periods of your time so have larger biological incentive to develop patterns of emotional feeding, that puts them in danger for semipermanent adverse health consequences like weight gain or upset.

Macht (2008) delineated a five-way model to elucidate the reasoning behind nerve-wracking eating: (1) emotional management of food selection, (2) emotional suppression of food intake, (3) impairment of psychological feature feeding controls, (4) feeding to control emotions, and (5) emotion-congruent modulation of feeding. These break down into subgroups of: header, reward improvement, social and conformity motive. Thus, providing a personal with are stronger understanding of private emotional feeding.

Positive have an effect on

Geliebter and Aversa (2003) conducted a study scrutiny people of 3 weight groups: weedy, traditional weight and overweight. each positive and negative emotions were evaluated. once people were experiencing positive emotional states or things, the weedy cluster coverage feeding over the opposite 2 teams. As a proof, the everyday nature of weedy people is to eat less and through times of stress to eat even less. However, once positive emotional states or things arise, people are a lot of probably to indulge themselves with food.

Impact

Emotional feeding could qualify as avoidant header and/or emotion-focused coping. As header ways that fall into these broad classes target temporary reprieve instead of sensible resolution of stressors, they'll initiate a vicious circle of maladjustive behavior bolstered by fugitive relief from stress. In addition, within the presence of high insulin levels characteristic of the recovery section of the stress-response, glucocorticoids trigger the creation of associate catalyst that stores away the nutrients current within the blood once an episode of emotional feeding as visceral fat, or fat set within the abdominal space. thus, those that struggle with emotional feeding are at larger risk for abdominal fatness, that is successively coupled to a larger risk for metabolic and upset.

Treatment

There are various ways in which during which people will scale back emotional distress while not partaking in emotional feeding as a way to cope. the foremost salient selection is to reduce maladjustive header ways and to maximize the adaptive strategies. A study conducted by Corstorphine et al. in 2007 investigated the link between distress tolerance and disordered feeding. These researchers specifically targeted on however completely different header ways impact distress tolerance and disordered feeding. They found that people who have interacted in disordered feeding usually use emotional shunning ways. If a personal is round-faced with robust negative emotions, they will favor to avoid true by distracting themselves through mortal sin. Discouraging emotional shunning is so a very important aspect to emotional feeding treatment. the foremost obvious thanks to limit emotional shunning is to confront {the issue|the difficulty|the drawback} through techniques like problem finding. Corstorphine et al. showed that people who have engaged in drawback finding ways enhance one's ability to tolerate emotional distress.Since emotional distress is correlative to emotional feeding, the power to raised manage one's negative have an effect on ought to permit a personal to deal with a state of affairs while not resorting to mortal sin.

One way to combat emotional feeding is to use attentiveness techniques. For instance, approaching cravings with a nonjudgmental curiosity will facilitate differentiate between hunger and emotionally-driven cravings. a personal could raise his or herself if the desire developed chop-chop, as emotional feeding tends to be triggered ad lib. a personal may additionally take the time to notice his or her bodily sensations, like hunger pangs, and coinciding emotions, like guilt or shame, so as to form aware choices to avoid emotional feeding.

Emotional feeding may be improved by evaluating physical aspects like secretion balance. feminine hormones, above all, will alter cravings and even self-perception of one's body. in addition, emotional feeding will be exacerbated by social pressure to be skinny. the main target on thinness and fasting in our culture will create young women, especially, at risk of falling into food restriction and subsequent emotional feeding behavior.

Emotional upset predisposes people to a lot of serious feeding disorders and physiological complications. Therefore, combatting disordered feeding before such progression takes place has become the main target of the many clinical psychologists.

EMOTIONAL

EATING

Break the Cycle, Say STOP Binge Eating! A Proven 21-Day Program Based on Ten Intuitive Principles for a Healthy Relationship with Food. Be Free from the Slavery of Hunger (Part 2)

By

Kelly Francis

professional before attempting any techniques outlined in this book.

By reading this document, the reader agrees that under no circumstances is the author responsible for any losses, direct or indirect, which are incurred as a result of the use of information contained within this document, including, but not limited to, — errors, omissions, or inaccuracies.

INTRODUCTION

Emotional Eating: Break the Cycle, Say STOP Binge Eating! A Proven-Effective 21-Day Program Based On Ten Intuitive Principles For A Healthy Relationship With Food. Find Freedom From Dieting Forever. Emotional eating is described as "the urge to eat in reaction to positive and negative feelings." While the word emotional eating mostly applies to eating as a means of coping with negative emotions, it also includes eating for positive emotions, such as eating food while enjoying an accomplishment or eating to boost an already good mood. Emotions often guide the feeding in these conditions but not in a negative way.

Any people get to terms with difficult situations by having comfort food. Chowing on ice cream or macaroni, and cheese will make it look like it's all right. And maybe there is an explanation why.

As points out, parts of the brain are punished with eating high-fat or high-sugar items. And more than a decade of psychological research shows that any rewarding activity would possibly replicate itself.

Emotional feeding means eating for purposes other than hunger. You can eat for being unhappy, upset, tired or lonely. Or you could be using food as a reward. Nutrition will find you relaxing and divert you from what really does concern you.

Eating comfort food as things get tough — also recognized as emotional eating or eating stress — is not, though, an answer to the challenges of life. It only works briefly. Worse, if it brings on weight gain, it creates longer-term anxiety.

Knowing what causes your emotional eating: Another way to control emotional eating is to find out what the symptoms are. Keep a food diary that not only tracks what you eat and how much but also how you felt at the time.

When you identify a trend, build a turnaround plan. For starters, if you often eat because you believe after a bad day you deserve it, realize that you also deserve to lose weight, feel healthy and be proud of yourself. If you are eating because of tension, learn to turn the discomfort down. Yoga, meditation and regular exercise may help to lower levels of stress.

Reasons of emotional eating: When finding out why you need comfort food you may be able to stop panic eating or emotional eating. Is it calming you down, cheering you up, making up for a bad day or a combination? Recognizing such patterns of thought can promote resistance to giving in. It also helps to understand that emotional eating is not solving the problem that led you to get angry.

The greatest breaks from emotional eating are activities that only require about five minutes switching gears— just long enough to help.

Several suggestions for moving strategies include: walking outside for a five-minute walk, turning on your favorite music and dancing, contacting a close friend to talk. The more ways you will think about entertaining yourself, the better it will become to stop eating tension over time. Instead it will become your new habit of fighting.

If you're an emotional eater, you may not notice the inherent signs of appetite and fullness in your body. You should eat more than you need or wish for.Emotional eating may interfere with making healthy choices regarding food. And it can keep you from getting to and remaining at a healthy weight.

What are symptoms of mental sustenance?

Everybody feeds from time to time, for purposes other than thirst. But if you find that out of hunger or for relaxation you sometimes search for food, you may be consuming for emotional reasons.

Common signs of emotional eating are: if you have more stress in your life, adjust your eating habits.
Feed if you're not thirsty, or are full.
Eating to soothe feelings.
Meat is used as a compliment.
Eating so as not to contend with a stressful situation.

Identify the emotional eating symptoms
One way to find out what emotional eating causes is to keep a diary of food. Factor in when and what you're doing. Write down also what you do and felt before you started eating. To find patterns in your eating habits, you can use this knowledge. For starters, you might find that you purchase an unhealthy snack from the office vending machine any time you start thinking about an assignment at work.

Use a scale of hunger: A scale of hunger will help you learn how to tell the difference between real, actual hunger and hunger in your mind. Psychological appetite is an eating impulse triggered by feelings, such as pain, anxiety, disappointment, or joy.

Value your appetite on a scale of 1 to 10 as you start feeling like you want something to eat, with 1 starving and 10 being so loaded you feel sick. A 5 or 6 rating means that you're comfortable— neither too hungry nor too whole.

Emotional eating is a form of reducing or relaxing negative emotions, such as tension, rage, anxiety, depression, sorrow and loneliness. Major events in life or, more generally, the daily life hassles may cause negative emotions that contribute to emotional eating and hinder the attempts to lose weight.

1—Starving, exhausted, dizzy 2—Very thin, cranky, low-energy, plenty of stomach rumbling 3—Pretty tired, stomach rumbling a little 4—Starting to feel a little better 5—Satisfied, neither hungry nor complete 6—A little full, comfortably full 7—A little awkward 8—Feeling bloated 9—Very cramped, stomach hurts 10—So loaded you feel sick

Use the scale to evaluate your appetite. If you feel like eating but your degree of hunger is a scale 6 or higher, pause and test your emotions.

Unpleasant eating happens when the diet becomes the reaction of an individual to certain unpleasant internal or external signals. The emotional eater may consume comfort foods rather than dealing in their thoughts and the stress they put in in an effort to distract themselves from the pain. This also includes, in most situations, a form of compulsive overeating that results in an overly full stomach sensation. Of reality, consuming this sort of food does not come without negative side effects. Three of the most famous are in the order.

Weight-related health concerns: Depression, high blood pressure, exhaustion and high cholesterol are all health issues that may come from frequent emotional eating outbursts.

Guilt: They're usually filled with guilt and shame for what they've done after the emotional "threat" has passed and the emotional overeater has eaten up. This guilt may contribute to another episode of emotional eating or low self-esteem.

Diarrhea: As nervous eaters often over-eat or eat too fast and suffer stomach pain or diarrhea afterwards, because the sight of food in the stomach acts as a diversion to the feelings they are trying to avoid. It can last a day or two after the actual meal.

We don't forever eat simply to satisfy physical hunger. several folks conjointly communicate food for comfort, stress relief, or to reward ourselves. And after we do, we tend to tend to succeed in for food, sweets, and different comforting however unhealthy foods. you may reach for a pint of frozen dessert once you're feeling down, order a pizza pie if you're bored or lonely, or swing by the drive-through once a nerve-wracking day at work. Emotional feeding is exploitation food to form yourself feel better—to fill emotional desires, instead of your abdomen. sadly, emotional feeding doesn't fix emotional issues. In fact, it always causes you to feel worse. Afterward, not solely will the first emotional issue stay, however you furthermore mght feel guilty for mortal sin.

People who showing emotion eat reach for food many times every week or a lot of to suppress and soothe negative feelings. they will even feel guilt or shame once feeding this manner, resulting in a cycle of excess feeding and associated problems, like weight gain.

The emotional feeding cycle

Occasionally exploitation food as a pick-me-up, a reward, or to celebrate isn't essentially a nasty factor. however once feeding is your primary emotional header mechanism— when your 1st impulse is to open the white goods whenever you're stressed, upset, angry, lonely, exhausted, or bored— you grind to a halt in an unhealthy cycle wherever the important feeling or drawback is rarely addressed .

Emotional hunger can't be crammed with food. feeding could feel sensible within the moment, however the sentiments that triggered the feeding are still there. And you regularly feel worse than you probably did before owing to the uncalled-for calories you've simply consumed. You beat yourself for messing up and not having a lot of resolution.

Compounding the matter, you stop learning healthier ways in which to upset your emotions, you've got a more durable and harder time dominant your weight, and you are feeling more and more overcome over each food and your feelings. however in spite of however overcome you are feeling over food and your feelings, it's potential to form a positive amendment. you'll be able to learn healthier ways in which to upset your emotions, avoid triggers, conquer cravings, and at last place a stop to emotional feeding.

The distinction between emotional hunger and physical hunger

Before you'll be able to become independent from from the cycle of emotional feeding, you initially got to learn the way to differentiate between emotional and physical hunger. this will be trickier than it sounds, particularly if you frequently use food to upset your feelings.

Emotional hunger will be powerful, thus it's simple to mistake it for physical hunger. however there are clues you'll be able to seek for to assist you tell physical and emotional hunger apart.

Emotional hunger comes on suddenly. It hits you in an immediate and feels overwhelming and pressing. Physical hunger, on the opposite hand, comes on a lot of bit by bit.

The urge to eat doesn't feel as dire or demand instant satisfaction (unless you haven't ingested for a awfully long time).

Emotional hunger craves specific comfort foods. once you're physically hungry, nearly something sounds good—including healthy stuff like vegetables. however emotional hunger craves food or sugar-coated snacks that offer an immediate rush. you are feeling such as you would like cheesecake or pizza pie, and zilch else can do.

Emotional hunger usually results in mindless feeding. Before you recognize it, you've ingested an entire bag of chips or an entire pint of frozen dessert while not extremely listening or totally enjoying it. once you're feeding in response to physical hunger, you're usually a lot of awake to what you're doing.

Emotional hunger isn't glad once you're full. you retain wanting a lot of and more, usually feeding till you're uncomfortably stuffed. Physical hunger, on the opposite hand, doesn't got to be stuffed. you are feeling glad once your abdomen is full.

Emotional hunger isn't set within the abdomen. instead of a growling belly or a pang in your abdomen, you are feeling your hunger as a desire you can't get out of your head. You're targeted on specific textures, tastes, and smells.

Emotional hunger usually results in regret, guilt, or shame. after you eat to satisfy physical hunger, you're unlikely to feel guilty or mortified as a result of you're merely giving your body what it desires. If you are feeling guilty once you eat, it's probably as a result of you recognize at bottom that you're not feeding for organic process reasons.

Emotional hunger vs. Physical hunger

Emotional hunger comes on suddenly Physical hunger comes on bit by bit

Emotional hunger looks like it must be glad instantly Physical hunger will wait

Emotional hunger craves specific comfort foods Physical hunger is receptive options—lots of things sound sensible

Emotional hunger isn't glad with a full abdomen. Physical hunger stops once you're full

Emotional feeding triggers feelings of guilt, quality, and shame feeding to satisfy physical hunger doesn't cause you to feel dangerous regarding yourself

Identify your emotional feeding triggers

The first step in putt a stop to emotional feeding is distinctive your personal triggers. What things, places, or feelings cause you to reach for the comfort of food? Most emotional feeding is coupled to unpleasant feelings, however it may be triggered by positive emotions, like appreciated yourself for achieving a goal or celebrating a vacation or blessed event.

CHAPTER 6:

A Simple List of Healthy Living Activities

We have all detected that having healthy habits like feeding well, staying active, and staying on prime of our health screenings is admittedly necessary.

But have you ever ever very considered why these items are therefore necessary, and the way all of them work together?

The good news is it's not onerous to make healthy, positive activities into your life. notwithstanding however previous you're or how unhealthy your former habits are, you'll be able to consistently introduce tiny changes into what you are doing daily.

Sometimes we are able to check out of management once it involves feeding. we tend to feel compelled to travel on craze diets, or total further onerous at the athletic facility. though it's important to exercise and watch what you eat, it's equally imperative that you just build an honest relationship with food. this could confirm the standard of your life--both at work and reception. Having a healthy relationship with food takes effort however operating towards feeling additional dead with feeding is well worthwhile. Here's what you'll be able to waste order to forestall unhealthy habits from continued.

Be versatile

"Our minds like to suppose in black-and-white terms," says Susan abstract artist, author of fifty ways that to appease Yourself while not Food. "Right versus wrong. Fat versus skinny. excellent versus ruined." If you don a diet, don't let yourself mentally spiral. once this happens, you may end up overthinking, overeating, and even basic cognitive process all types of negative thoughts and judgments regarding yourself. think about being less strict with what you eat. abstract artist advises to even often break your diet--even simply a bit bit--because being versatile will relieve a lot of of the strain you will feel. And, as she notes, "When you see that nothing unhealthy happens, flexibility won't be as discouraging. you may even relish it."

Be attentive.

When does one stuff or eat unhealthy food? will a particular event or feeling trigger your unhealthy feeding habits? typically, for instance, we crave bound foods once we are bored at work, and that we head to the slot machine to resolve the desire. Be aware of your hunger triggers and cues--when you finally notice and concentrate to your unhealthy feeding patterns, you'll be able to effectively dismantle them.

Be relaxed

Keep a relaxed approach once it involves food--not solely will this facilitate with weight maintenance however it conjointly helps you create progress along with your health overall. Relaxed feeding helps you eat till you're nutritionally happy and helps ease emotional eating, therefore think about swiftness down throughout all meals --even lunch at your table. Examine the various textures, tastes, and elements of your food, and higher than all-- enjoy.

What Are Healthy Habits?

A healthy habit is any activity or behavior that may profit your physical, mental, or emotional well-being. At first, these tiny changes may not appear that effective. however once place along dozens of those little habits you'll be able to produce a framework for a healthy life.

It is very important to recollect that healthy habits is created little by little. What may be associate degree unhealthy habit for one person nowadays may be a healthy habit for somebody else.

For example, fake you've got associate degree unhealthy habit of feeding 2 bowls of frozen dessert nightly. Cutting this all the way down to one bowl or perhaps simply 0.5 a bowl is creating progress towards the healthy habit of reducing on unhealthy food. However, for somebody who doesn't eat these foods to start with, feeding a bowl of frozen dessert an evening wouldn't be thought of a healthy habit.

Start wherever you're and build progress towards habits which will be healthy for you.

In this list of healthy habits, you may study feeding higher, exercising, associate degreed having an overall healthy fashion.

While some might not apply to any or all folks, these habits are an excellent start line for anyone who is also trying to raised themselves.

Physical Activity (Fitness)

Getting physical activity edges each your body and your mind. It helps keep your weight up to speed, fights off chronic diseases, reduces stress, improves your mood, and provides you a way of accomplishment.

Getting physical activity doesn't got to involve hours at the athletic facility. Instead, there are many ways that you just will make tiny changes throughout the day to form your life less inactive and acquire your body moving.

You can even involve your friends or family in your physical activity therefore you'll be able to have your time to act with the folks you're keen on while conjointly benefiting your body. There are numerous forms of physical activities that you just may boost your day, it's simply necessary to search out one that you just relish and continue it.

1. Do housekeeping.

2. Take 30-minute early morning walks.

3. Implement the two-minute walking habit for each hour that you just sit.

4. Take the steps rather than the elevator.

5. Walk whenever you'll be able to.

6. Use a treadmill table.

7. Use a height-adjustable table.

8. Aim for 10,000 steps each day. Wear a step-tracking device.

9. Take a dance break.

10. Go hiking additional usually.

11. Do yoga.

12. Go mountain climbing.

13. Go geocaching.

14. exercise throughout TV commercials.

15. Do some Deskercise.

What are the healthiest habits to feature to your routine? Getting physical activity doesn't got to involve hours at the athletic facility. Take a dance break!

Forgiveness (Healthy Lifestyle)

While forgiveness could seem like an antediluvian notion of our rush and quick-to-react society, there are several health edges thereto, even today.

When you are consciously able to let one thing go, even while not associate degree apology, it reduces your anger, stress, and tension.

The physical burden of feeling hurt takes a toll on the body, therefore having the ability to unharness those negative feelings and replace them with quality may be a healthy habit.

Choosing to not forgive somebody will increase your anger and contributes to a sense of loss of management. Holding onto a grudge will increase muscle tension, heart rate, and pressure level, that are all harmful to your health.

Being able to forgive somebody also will improve your sleep. you may not pay time lying in bed in the dead of night ruminating over one thing that happened within the past, or coming up with what quite return you wish to form. If you'll be able to meditate and totally forgive somebody else, you'll be able to focus additional on you and your own well-being. Finally, having the ability to forgive will strengthen your relationship along with your friends and family. Avoiding deep-seeded strains in shut relationships is a crucial a part of feeling connected to those around you and living life harmonical with folks that cross your path. Maintaining healthy relationships may be a key part of living a healthy fashion.

16. Don't move to sleep angry.

17. specialise in understanding yourself rather than blaming others.

18. board this rather than being stuck within the past.

19. get it on for yourself and your own peace of mind.

20. keep in mind the days after you were forgiven.

21. keep in mind folks once they were kids.

22. keep in mind why you're keen on folks.

23. keep in mind that it's higher to be kind rather than right.

24. Observe, don't decide.

25. Take responsibility for your own shortcomings.

26. Acknowledge your growth from the expertise.

Portion Size management (Healthy Eating)

Sometimes, it isn't what you eat, however what quantity of it you're feeding.

For example, avocados are very healthy and have loads to supply in terms of nutrients and healthy fats. However, they're terribly dense in calories, therefore feeding 3 avocados per day wouldn't be a healthy habit.

Eat till you're physically happy, and so stop. If you're thinking that you will still be hungry, wait twenty minutes, drink a glass of water, and rethink if you actually want another serving to.

Also, begin feeding on smaller plates therefore you're feeling as if your plate is full before you sit all the way down to a meal. you may most likely be shocked at the number of food that really accounts for a serving size.

Remember that feeding isn't a pursuit or one thing to try to to after you are bored or wired. confirm you're advertently feeding once it's time to try to to therefore, which you sit down and solely specialise in your food.

Mindlessly feeding ahead of the tv or running to the white goods if you've got had a nasty day are each bad eating habits that cause additional health issues down the road.

27. Avoid feeding once feeling stressed.

28. Use portion-control containers to store your meals.

29. Use portion-control plates once feeding reception.

30. hear your hunger cues.

31. Drink many water and healthy fluids.

32. Keep a food diary or journal.

33. build and drink healthy smoothies.

34. find out how to browse nutrition labels.

35. be from fun-size candy bars and alternative treats.

36. arrange your meals each week.

37. build your own single-serving snack packs.

38. Limit distractions throughout meal times.

39. Take probiotics daily

40. keep on with your grocery list.

41. strive turmeric supplements

42. Take smaller bites and eat slowly.

43. Chew your food a minimum of 5 times before swallowing.

44. Drink before you get thirsty.

healthy living quotes - "An over-indulgence of something, even one thing as pure as water, will intoxicate." —Criss Jami

Preventive Health Care Screening

People tend to travel to the doctor once they become unwell, or once an unacquainted symptom pops up. From there, the doctor works with the patient to treat the matter in hopes that it'll flee. however what if the matter ne'er happened within the 1st place?

For example, if you notice alittle mark on your skin that has ostensibly popped up out of obscurity and you don't understand what it's, this might be a proof of carcinoma that may chop-chop unfold throughout your body. Don't ignore these items and hope they're going to flee. Instead, be proactive and visit a medical specialist each year to induce checkups in order that they will look over your skin for love or money that they'll realize suspicious.

It is necessary to be proactive regarding your health, despite if you're sick or not. Doctors could provide recommendation on preventative measures for diseases that run in your family, or perhaps simply catch a unhealthiness before it becomes too late. Catching health problems early is that the key, therefore confirm that you just are listening to your physical health notwithstanding however you really feel.

43. Annual physical test.

44. Thyroid take a look at (for girls only).

45. Bone mineral density take a look at (women).

46. X ray (women).

47. endoscopy.

48. abstinence plasma aldohexose take a look at.

49. Eye exam.

50. Hearing take a look at.

51. Dental test and improvement.

52. Abdominal aneurism screening (for men only).

53. pressure level screening.

54. sterol screening.

55. Prostate screening (men).

56. carcinoma screening.

57. gonad self-exam (men).

58. Pap test and HPV test (women).

59. Chlamydia take a look at (women).

60. Venus's curse take a look at (women).

61. HIV take a look at and alternative sexually transmitted infection tests.

62. Skin exams.

63. respiratory illness (flu) immunogen.

64. viral hepatitis immunogen.

65. viral hepatitis immunogen.

66. Herpes shingles immunogen.

67. Human papillomavirus (HPV) immunogen.

68. MMR (measles, mumps, rubella).

69. Meningococcal (meningitis).

70. respiratory disorder immunogen.

71. Tetanus, diphtheria, pertussis.

72. chickenpox (chicken pox).

Suggested Timeline for Routine Health Screening

Schedule for men:

Physical exam: each 2 to a few years for men eighteen and over.

Colonoscopy: each 7-10 years for men fifty and over.

Eye exam: One before the age of thirty, as suggested by a doctor when age forty, each one to 2 years when age sixty five.

Hearing test: Once each ten years for men ages 18-50, once each three years for men fifty one and over.

Dental cleaning: double a year for men over eighteen.

Blood pressure screening: each 2 years when the age of eighteen.

Cholesterol screening: each 5 years beginning at age thirty five.

Prostate screening: starting at age fifty.

Skin exam: Yearly, starting at the age of eighteen.

Schedule for women

Physical exam: Annual.

Bone mineral density test: starting at age sixty five.

Mammogram: each one to 2 years beginning at age forty.

Clinical breast exam: each 3 years for ladies Which are 20-40.

Colonoscopy: each 7-10 years for ladies fifty and over.

Fasting plasma aldohexose test: each 3 years starting at age forty five.

Eye exam: One before the age of thirty, as suggested by a doctor when age forty, each one to 2 years when age sixty five.

Dental cleaning: double a year for ladies over eighteen.

Blood pressure screening: each 2 years starting at the age of eighteen.

Cholesterol screening: each 5 years beginning at age thirty five.

Pap test: each 3 years for ladies ages 21-29, each 5 years for ladies 30-65, testing is also discontinued at age sixty five if no previous issues have occurred.

Skin exam: Yearly when the age of eighteen.

Adequate Sleep (Healthy Living)

Sleep plays a awfully necessary role in maintaining general well-being and a healthy fashion. obtaining enough deep sleep in the dead of night will facilitate shield your mental and physical health, your overall quality of life, and your safety.

How you're feeling whereas you're awake is greatly addicted to the standard of sleep you're accessing night. whereas you're sleeping, your body is replenishing itself to support healthy brain perform and optimize your physical health.

Sleep conjointly plays an outsized role within the growth and development of youngsters.

Sleep deficiency will happen each quickly and over time. If you're losing sleep on a daily basis, you will raise your risk for chronic health issues, expertise hassle thinking throughout the day, have delayed reactions, have poor performance at work, expertise learning difficulties, and have issues developing relationships.

If you are doing not provide your body an opportunity to revive itself from expenditure energy all day and prepare itself for the energy you may want the subsequent day, your health will definitely suffer.

73. Avoid alkaloid within the afternoon.

74. Avoid significant meals on the brink of time of day.

75. Keep your pets out of the bed.

76. Be consistent in your sleep schedule.

77. Don't drink too several fluids before bed.

78. Quit smoking.

79. Set your temperature between 60-67 degrees F.

80. Shut off natural philosophy a minimum of associate degree hour before bed.

81. Wear socks.

82. Get non secular.

83. Visualize. suppose happy thoughts.

84. Keep a sleep log.

85. Have a wind-down sleep routine.

86. find out how to induce back to sleep.

87. confirm that the space is dark and quiet.

88. Use an important oil diffuser with the correct volatile oil for sleep.

These healthy habits for adults will assist you start on healthy living and quit smoking.

Give yourself the possibility to sleep higher b quitting smoking and alternative habit-forming substances.

Try one thing New

Everyone gets into a typical routine wherever they are doing constant factor just about a day. However, there are many ways to combine up your schedule a touch therefore you'll be able to strive new things. dynamic your routine can assist you challenge yourself and learn new things.

If you're hesitant initially, you will find yourself shocked at what quantity you relish your new activity or the new folks you meet. making an attempt new things can result in multiplied confidence and a better level of shallowness, whereas conjointly reducing dissatisfaction and loneliness. this may facilitate drive your personal growth, improve your health, and increase longevity.

89. Learn a replacement language.

90. Watch a far off language film (with subtitles, of course).

91. strive feeding at a replacement edifice. Let the waiter perceive your meal.

92. visit somewhere you've ne'er been before.

93. sign on and attend a category associated with your work.

94. strive a replacement sport.

95. Cook a straightforward meal you've ne'er tried before.

96. Take a distinct route to figure, or get there during a new method.

97. Take a road trip.

98. strive a replacement look.

99. hear a replacement (to you) genre of music.

100. browse a book from an author you've ne'er detected of.

101. strive a replacement sort of exercise.

102. Watch a replacement play or musical.

103. Watch a tangle show.

104. Go one week while not web.

105. Go one weekend while not payment.

Strength and adaptability (Fitness)

Your muscles naturally lose strength and reduce in size with age. they're going to doubtless conjointly diminish supple and stiffer. These changes will have an effect on your vary of movement in your joints and cause you to lose tissue snap, which can result in tight muscles.

One of the most reasons that muscles begin to weaken and lose flexibility is inactivity. while not doing strength-building and adaptability exercises, the loss of flexibility could result in permanent harm in your posture and loss of healthy muscle perform. it's so imperative to take care of muscle flexibility as a crucial part of overall fitness.

Having versatile muscles helps to scale back any soreness in your body, and to enhance your posture. Stretching may improve your muscular balance by realigning the tissues in your body, which can cut back the hassle that's required to take care of balance. With robust muscles and adaptability, you may have a diminished risk of injury and a bigger vary of motion.

Finally, active these healthy habits can increase the blood and nutrients that are delivered to the tissues throughout your body. this is often as a result of, after you stretch, you're increasing the temperature of your tissues, that then will increase your circulation and also the transportation of nutrients.

106. Pushups.

107. Crunches.

108. Curl to press.

109. Fly to tris.

110. Lying march.

111. Ball squat.

112. Dips.

113. Tripod row.

114. Shoulder and chest.

115. Arm across chest.

116. striated muscle stretch.

117. striated muscle stretch.

118. skeletal muscle stretch.

119. Single leg hamstring.

120. Standing musculus quadriceps femoris.

healthy fashion quotes - "A work, healthy body—that is that the best fashion statement." —Jess C. Scott

Laugh (Healthy Living)

Some researchers believe that laughter very may be the most effective medication, as a result of it will assist you feel higher and cut back stress. Having a positive angle, being receptive property loose, and having an honest sense of humor also will assist you to develop relationships with people and kind robust bonds.

Studies have truly found that once folks laugh, their brains bear constant changes that they are doing once folks are advertently meditating. This makes folks feel invigorated and prepared to beat issues that they run into throughout the day. The therapeutic worth of laughter remains being studied, but so far, it's solely shown positive results.

121. Learn the therapeutic edges of laughter.

122. plan to happy additional.

123. Watch silly TV shows and flicks.

124. think about finding out a laughter yoga club.

125. be part of a laughter-based exercise program.

126. interact in voluntary, self-initiated laughter.

127. Schedule time to look at funny videos on YouTube.

128. pay longer along with your pets.

129. browse funny books or newspaper comics.

130. Have a favourite comedian.

131. Watch a stand-up comedy show live or on YouTube.

132. hear funny podcasts.

133. join up with previous friends and remember.

134. Visit associate degree common.

135. look into your previous footage.

Family and Friends (Healthy Lifestyle)

We aren't created to measure alone. we tend to are born with our mothers, and quite probably alternative encompassing relations. Throughout numerous stages of life, we rely on people to assist us accomplish things on the method.

In order to try to to most something, you've got to own some kind of cooperation of people. Humans have evolved to collaborate so as to survive. Having each family and friends that you just will consider, turn to, and socialize with can provide you with a way of happiness and permit you to relate to folks that share your values and beliefs.

A very necessary a part of self-care is to form it a priority to develop and maintain human relationships. typically it takes effort throughout our busy lives to stay up-to-date with all of our loved ones, however it's a awfully healthy habit to try to to therefore.

136. build it some extent to eat dinner along as a family.

137. Schedule a weekly family night.

138. Schedule yearly family vacations.

139. Exercise, do chores, and play along.

140. browse time of day stories to young children, and share books with older ones.

141. Keep and still grow your family ikon albums.

142. Get to understand your children's friends.

143. facilitate your children with schoolwork.

144. Go bivouacking along.

145. Bring your children to high school.

146. Leave love or encouraging notes.

147. Work on common goals with (a) friend(s). Be every other's responsibility partner.

148. Host a affair.

149. arrange a reading date along with your friend(s).

150. facilitate your friends with chores.

151. join up with friends for lunch a minimum of once a month.

It's a healthy habit to stay up-to-date with all of our loved ones. build it a priority to develop and maintain human relationships.

Maintaining healthy relationships is one amongst the healthy habits for adults and healthy habits for all times.

Address habit-forming Behaviors

When you accept the word "addiction," you will solely think about alcohol, tobacco, and drug use.

However, there are alternative behaviors that will be healthy sparsely, however that may find yourself turning into addictions. Things like food, caffeine, web usage, and gambling will all become habit-forming for a few folks.

There are safe levels for these forms of behaviors, and that we have to be compelled to acknowledge and address our habits so as to understand once they are in excess. it's necessary to contemplate your temperament once doing this. Studies have shown that there are connections between unthoughtfulness, compulsivity, and addiction.

You have to be able to self-reflect to visualize if you've got any repetitive behaviors that you just do while not a rational motivation.

A full-blown addiction happens after you have associate degree inability to prevent a harmful behavior even if it's negative consequences. If you see a retardant, it's necessary to act to handle the problem.

152. begin by admitting that you just have a retardant.

153. perceive the implications of your habit-forming behavior.

154. Assess however unhealthy your habit-forming behavior is.

155. understand and think about your temperament.

156. Discover what's driving the behavior.

157. perceive your habit loop. establish your triggers. find out how to interrupt unhealthy habits.

158. interact during a new, totally different routine that disrupts your habit-forming behavior.

159. Keep associate degree responsibility journal. (like the liberty Journal)

160. Reward yourself.

161. If you're feeling you wish skilled facilitate, think about seeing a healer.

Quiet Your Mind (Healthy Living)

Taking your time out of the day to quiet your mind and meditate may be a good way to scale back stress. It will assist you connect your body along with your mind and unharness any settled tension from things that are happening in your personal or business life.

This will conjointly provide you with an opportunity to replicate on something happening in your life, and settle for or touch upon issues that are keeping you from being no-hit or achieving your goals. Your mind wants rest throughout the day therefore it is able to strive against ensuing task that comes your method.

162. apply a morning respiration exercise.

163. produce AN "if-then" arrange for times once monkey mind starts to induce the higher of you.

164. apply morning meditation.

165. apply shower meditation.

166. Be an observer of your own thoughts.

167. apply pranayama.

168. apply qigong.

169. begin a journal or write your "morning pages."

170. produce a tea or occasional ritual.

171. apply yoga.

172. Recite mantras or positive affirmations.

173. Build focus.

174. apply aware feeding.

175. Take a digital break often.

176. Take a music break.

177. Decrease distractions.

Gratitude

Reminding yourself what you're grateful for every day can facilitate keep your spirits up and ward off any lingering depression. specialise in the positives in your life instead of the negatives, and keep your strengths in mind as you begin day after day.Making this deliberate purpose of being appreciative for everything you've got in your life is helpful for your happiness and overall well-being. typically we tend to forget the little things that we regard granted a day that we truly wouldn't understand what to try to to while not.

178. Keep a feeling journal.

179. provide a minimum of one compliment a day.

180. Say many thanks

181. Say grace before meals.

182. every morning, think about a minimum of 3 belongings you are grateful for.

183. Smile additional usually.

184. Volunteer for organizations or causes you think in.

185. Write an acquaintance, relative or new acquaintance a many thanks note for being a part of your life.

186. build a feeling collage.

187. Appreciate nature.

188. Listen actively once somebody else is talking.

189. Write and send a many thanks notes.

190. "Look for the helpers." – Fred Rogers

191. Be appreciative after you learn one thing new.

192. Reward effort.

These final list of fine habits for a healthy life embody feeling and spoken communication many thanks as key to a pregnant healthy fashion.

Reminding yourself what you're grateful for every day can facilitate keep your spirits up and ward off any lingering depression.

When you apply healthy habits, you increase your probabilities of living a extended and healthier life. though you begin tiny, you'll be able to considerably cut back your probabilities of developing a chronic unwellness or dying untimely compared with those that apply solely unhealthy habits.

Bad habits could definitely be troublesome to interrupt, however once you're able to get within the routine of active healthy habits, you may not regret your call to form the hassle. whereas your behavioural changes might not occur long, it's necessary to wait and take tiny steps someday at a time.

I hope you enjoyed this in depth list of healthy habits. I hope you're not fazed by the sheer variety of tasks needed to measure a healthy fashion. it's loads, however we tend to don't have to be compelled to be one hundred pc excellent all the time.

If you acknowledge the importance of those healthy habits and do your personal best to incrementally improve you're leagues before those that don't have any plan what healthy living is all regarding.

try these fourteen tips to push durable weight loss and acquire healthier overall—there are numerous edges besides probably nudging the quantity on the scale!

1. concentrate to your parts.

"Most Americans eat 2 to a few times the particular serving size of foods," says Mashru. It doesn't facilitate that restaurants usually serve huge parts, which might train your mind to suppose that's the number of food your body wants. to induce a handle on correct serving sizes, Mashru suggests checking nutrition labels or Googling around to visualize what quantity of any given food counts as some for one person.

2. place your fork down between bites.

It helps you eat additional slowly, that may be a straightforward plan of action to chop back on calories. after you take some time rather than eupnoeic your food, your body will truly register the sensation of fullness, which might take up to twenty minutes to hit your brain. Plus, feeding slowly may even build your food style higher, in keeping with associate degree October 2015 study printed within the journal Proceedings of the National Academy of Sciences of the us of America. Wins all around.

3. drink water 24/7.

Even though your body is mostly a reasonably good machine, it is vulnerable to slip-ups. "Sometimes what you're thinking that may be a hunger pang is caused by thirst," says Zeitlin. That "hunger" will cause you to snack once all of your body needs is a few association. If you're not a lover of the plain stuff, strive these twelve straightforward ways to drink additional water.

4. Carve out time to organize your lunch.

Not solely can creating your own lunch assist you save cash, it'll make sure you understand precisely what you're golf stroke into your body which you're obtaining the correct nutrients. "You're conjointly less doubtless to skip lunch on busy days after you will simply walk to the refrigerator rather than having to travel out and buy," says Mashru. though it feels like skipping those calories may facilitate boost weight loss, depriving your body of normal meals simply causes you to additional doubtless to do it later.

5. Don't do alternative things whereas you're feeding.

It is powerful to specialise in feeding once there's work to try to to and Instagram to ascertain, however chowing down once you're distracted will result in accidentally taking in additional than you wish. Distracted feeding doesn't simply result in additional consumption within the moment, it will even compel you to eat quite necessary afterward within the day, in keeping with a scientific review of twenty four studies within the Feb 2013 edition of The yank Journal of Clinical Nutrition.

CHAPTER 7:

Foods That invariably price but forty Cents Per Serving

B uild breakfast a priority.

"Eating a breakfast jam-packed with lean supermolecule and fiber can keep you happy, that helps you create higher food decisions throughout the day," to maximise the ability of breakfast, take meals that aren't macromolecule bombs empty substantial to stay you full, like bagels, dry cereal, and muffins. "Try disorganized eggs on whole grain toast, plain Greek dairy product with a cup of your favorite fruit, or associate degree omelette loaded with veggies," says Zeitlin.

Be a sensible nosher.

When you're making an attempt to melt off, snacking will either be your best bud or a ostensibly useful, nonetheless undeniably sneaky saboteur. There's the problem of inadvertently taking in additional than you're thinking that,

that you'll be able to fix during a snap by pre-portioning your snacks in keeping with their serving sizes instead of simply chip away at them every which way. Another snacking drawback will arise if you graze, aka eat senselessly throughout the day, instead of snack advisedly. investigate these snacking for weight loss tips to form positive you're on the correct track.

8. Clock enough hours of sleep nightly.

It is onerous to stay to an honest sleep schedule—especially once there are episodes of state to catch up on—but obtaining enough rest is a simple thanks to encourage weight loss. "Sleep helps keep the appetency hormones hormone and leptin in restraint," "Without AN adequate quantity, those hormones become unbalanced and might result in an multiplied appetency." in keeping with the adults ought to aim for between seven and 9 hours an evening.

Keep on with healthy feeding even on the weekends.

When you're passionate about feeding well Monday through Fri however think about weekends a food scrap, you will not see the burden loss you expect. "If you add it up, feeding poorly and not exertion Fri to Sunday comes dead set twelve days 'off' a month!" says Mashru. "Instead of property the times of the week influence your habits, specialise in making a healthy lifestyle—with the occasional indulgence —that's property all month long."

Consider smaller plates.

If you look into constant quantity of food on a bit plate vs. an outsized one, your eyes may persuade you there's additional appetisingness on the smaller dish. this is often thanks to what's called the Delboeuf illusion, that shows that encompassing one thing during a heap of white area will build it look smaller. though you're not feeding a lot of, curtailing on the number of plate area around your food will trick your brain into thinking it's a much bigger portion than it very is, whereas doing the alternative could tend your hunger by creating you're thinking that you simply Greek deity a touch.

Trim on family vogue feeding.

When you dine with serving dishes jam-packed with further helpings right ahead of you, you'll be able to slip into senselessly filling your plate though you're not still hungry. Instead, whenever doable, limit the food on the table to what you're truly feeding. That's to not say seconds are forbidden—just that you just ought to sign in to visualize if you're still hungry before obtaining up to grab some additional.

Sit facing off from the buffet at restaurants.

Always having additional food in your line of sight could push you to induce into food-coma territory, particularly if you're making an attempt to induce your money's price.

instead of feeding whereas gazing at what you may treat yourself to next, flip your back to the opposite food and specialise in very enjoying what's on your plate. If you wish additional food once you're done, the buffet can still be there!

Pile your plate high with vegetables.

One of the most effective ways that to induce into the healthy-eating habit is by adding things to your diet rather than removing them. Refusing to eat any of your favorite treats will backfire during a binge, whereas slowly increasing your vegetable intake will solely bring smart results. "Not solely are vegetables crammed with necessary nutrients that keep your body healthy and energized, they contain fiber, that helps you're feeling surfeited," says Mashru. To avoid vegetable burnout, she suggests beginning small: add a cup of them to a minimum of one meal each day for per week, then begin incorporating them into additional meals as you get accustomed them.

Keep a food journal.

If you're doing all of the higher than however still not seeing any noticeable weight loss, dropping pounds will want a mysterious equation you only can't crack. in this case, Zeitlin suggests keeping a food journal therefore you've got a close nonetheless overarching read of your habits. "It will assist you realize the areas specific to you and your fashion that would use some tiny tweaking," she says. Do your best to trace your food and potable intake for per week, then recall to visualize if you're inadvertently taking during a few further calories you may cut get in order to induce the results you're when. Above all, keep in mind that losing weight healthily usually involves some trial and error—but the purpose is that on the method you find out how to be smart to your body, that is admittedly what matters.

The Next Healthy Habits you must Build

1. Drink a glass of water very first thing within the morning.

This health tip is easy, however conjointly quite necessary. Here are many reasons why this could be a part of your healthy consumption habits:

While sleeping, your body gets dehydrated. What it craves, and can be happy to receive as shortly as attainable, could be a whole glass of water. In giving that to your body, you'll feel instantly invigorated and can conjointly jump begin your metabolism. It seems, you don't essentially have to be compelled to eat breakfast super early, however you do need to place this supernatural liquid in your system in real time.

To make it even easier, place the glass next to your bed as a reminder. within the morning, fill it with water, add a lemon, and provides yourself concerning five minutes to totally fancy the method of provision your body and brain. build it a meditation! Why not?

Some a lot of advantages of this tiny trick are that it clears your mind and causes you to alert and totally awake. With that, you'll be able to simply begin the day, have a productive morning, and be a lot of centered than usual for the remainder of the day.

Water conjointly helps flush toxins out of the body, strengthens the system, and plays a large role in managing your weight.

Try doing this very first thing within the morning tomorrow and knowledge all of those positive effects for yourself!

CHAPTER 8:

Tiny Healthy habits

2. Leave technology behind within the evening

Most people have sleeping issues. However, it's crucial to induce your eight roughly hours of sleep nightly so as to possess energy and a transparent mind succeeding day. If you don't, your body and brain can suffer in many alternative ways that.

Some of the factors symptom your sleep are attending to bed together with your phone, browsing the net on your laptop computer, observance a pic to induce yourself to sleep, or checking social media and obtaining flooded. For this, victimisation technology before time of day has become a difficulty — it keeps your brain activated; no marvel you have got issues falling asleep.

There's a straightforward answer, and you must add it to your arsenal of daily healthy habits: undo an hour before bed.

Do it for simply ten minutes these days, or advice yourself you won't be taking your phone or laptop computer to bed any longer. Then, build this era of your time longer once you're feeling comfy with it.

It's most higher to travel to bed peacefully and be positive concerning tomorrow, instead of be unbroken awake considering the posts you simply browse on your friend's timeline, the unhealthy news you were bombarded with, or an argument you had on social media.

3. Forming healthy consumption habits with very little changes

You can modification your whole design over time by setting out to for a few little healthy consumption habits these days. for example, you'll be able to begin intense proteins and veggies with every meal. Then, your want for unhealthy foods can eventually get away, and you'll still feel full and happy once an enormous meal.

Soon after, you'll be able to add supplements like polyunsaturated fatty acid fatty acids to your daily diet. It's a little, 2-second act (taking the pills), however are some things which will boost your health in varied other ways. The krill/fish supplement is verified to regulate many sorts of diseases. As a bonus, it fights depression and anxiety, is sweet for your eyes and heart, and reduces inflammation.

4. Journal your thoughts

Journaling is on this list of health tips for many reasons.

First of all, it's another likelihood to remain far from technology and boost your psychological state by removal your mind and swing it all on paper. However, the good thing about this healthy habit goes abundant more.

By sharing your thoughts on paper, you're learning a way to open up. In real world, that creates your relationships better over time and you become a far better person.

It's nice for staying intended to achieve your goals. By writing concerning your goals, you visualize that it's already happening and your brain works to bring you the required circumstances in life to induce you nearer to it vision.

Journaling is additionally a medical care. you'll be able to write your fears and doubts, and feel higher after. It brings clarity and attentiveness to any or all problems you address.

5. Have stretch breaks

This one is for mental and physical health.

The truth is, we tend to work an excessive amount of and don't take breaks — whichs finishes up truly devastation our productivity.

Instead, our brain must be engaged in restful activities the maximum amount as once each hour. that may be as very little as five minutes of stretching, respiratory deeply, enjoying a cup of tea, and simply filling your mind with positive thoughts.

It's conjointly instructed to try and do correct stretching once you get up, and before you visit sleep. within the morning, stretching helps to induce the body get in active mode. within the evening, on the opposite hand, it helps your brain get into sleep mode and is a lot of of a soothing activity, instead of one transfer energy to any or all elements of your body.

6. begin walking

Sounds easy, right? Yet, we tend to avoid it the maximum amount as attainable. Well, currently can be the proper time in your life to feature walking to your daily healthy habits.

It's helpful for your physical well-being as by doing it daily, you're staying active. Also, it's nice for removal your mind, respiratory some contemporary air, obtaining some fat-soluble vitamin (if done throughout the day), and boosting your mood naturally and feeling a lot of alive!

Walking is additionally connected to stronger bones and lower vital sign. If you're not the kind of one that likes exercise, this can be the simplest variety of moving your body and still obtaining the advantages like losing body fat, doing basic cardio, and rising your heart health.

If you're questioning a way to embody it in your daily schedule, you'll be able to do this:

If you get up earlier, it may be an incredible begin of the day. You'll be intended to feature another healthy habits to your morning routine later on.

Even your lunch break may be your formula for achievement at work... If you are doing the proper activities throughout it. this can be as a result of it's necessary to fully shut your brain off and stop considering the items happening at the office; for this, you must do one thing completely different, and ideally outside. If you get out and simply walk, although it's for ten minutes, you'll see that the strain goes away, creating area for relaxation, attentiveness, and even creativeness. Once you're back to figure, you'll realize it easier to focus and can get a lot of done.

7. Prepare your food

If you wish to require care of your well-being, you must accept sensible foods. Don't simply ditch food, even be conscious of what you're fitting your body: live it, have mounted times for meals, and prepare it yourself.

This will all happen over time, of course. Such healthy consumption habits, however, can impact the remainder of your life. Researchers have found that home change of state results in healthier living.

But wait! There's a lot of...

You're building discipline by locution no to consumption on the go. you furthermore mght build have the benefit of shopping for groceries yourself and so obtaining artistic within the room. This method makes the meal one thing to appreciate— you build a brand new talent, track your intake, and therefore the food satisfies you far more currently that you've worked it.

You don't have to be compelled to get something that comes in a very package. Finally begin victimisation your room. You'll shortly begin researching a lot of health tips yourself, what ingredients to incorporate, a way to mix foods, etc.

Such a conscious preparation, and therefore the delicious meal that follows, are nice ways that to stay your relationship together with your loved ones, family, or roommates sturdy (they can love you!). Meals are an opportunity to bond, and consumption is far a lot of pleasant once it becomes a group action. No want for fancy restaurants — you're saving cash by change of state your food, too.

These healthy habits are going to be enough to alter your life in many ways. Begin these days. By shopping for polyunsaturated fatty acid, by swing a glass beside your bed, by journaling many thoughts, or by obtaining outside and walking round the neighborhood for ten minutes. . . you'll feel it.

To live healthy is simple. simply build these a part of your daily routine.

What works for one person might not work for succeeding.

When creating changes, some individuals (like me) choose to go all-in and alter everything at identical time.

But others like the longer, slower approach... creating little changes, one at a time.

Neither approach is healthier than the opposite, it's simply that individuals have completely different personalities and wish to approach mode changes otherwise.

It explains a way to adopt a healthy, real food based mostly diet in twelve easy, simply manageable steps.

You can do one step per week, one each fortnight, or one per month... whichever suits you. Waiting till you get accustomed one modification before creating succeeding could be a sensible plan.

Whatever you are doing, you must begin seeing results at once, as a result of every step will have a strong impact.

When you're through with this, you must have lost a major quantity of weight and improved your health, each physical and mental, in each method conceivable.

Remember... habit puts resolve on autopilot. Changes in mode and behavior may be robust within the starting, however become easy after you flip them into a habit.

By mastering one little habit at a time, you'll set yourself up for long success.

Here are steps to nutrition.

1. Eat a lot of macromolecule to spice up Your Metabolism and cut back Your appetency, creating Future Changes Easier

Before we tend to cipher, we add.

This initiative can modification your metabolism in a very method that creates resultant changes easier.

First of all, macromolecule truly boosts your rate... that is, what percentage calories you burn at rest.

The studies show that top macromolecule diets boost metabolism by eighty to a hundred calories per day, compared to low macromolecule diets.

Second of all, macromolecule will cut back your appetency, creating you mechanically eat less of alternative calorie

In one study, consumption macromolecule at 30% of calories caused an automatic reduction in calorie intake of 449 calories per day. The individuals lost four.9 weight unit (11 lbs) in twelve weeks, while not designedly limiting something,

Of course... adequate macromolecule conjointly has several alternative advantages, together with enlarged muscle mass, stronger bones, lower vital sign, to call many.

Good macromolecule sources embody meat, poultry, fish, seafood, eggs and full-fat dairy farm product (if you'll be able to tolerate them). Some individuals like beans and legumes, that are fully fine if properly ready.

I recommend consumption concerning one.5-2.5 grams of macromolecule per metric weight unit of bodyweight, or 0.7 -1.1 grams per pound.

You don't really want to weigh or live this, however it's going to be an honest plan to trace your foods within the setting out to ensure you're obtaining enough.

Eating a lot of macromolecule is that the best, simplest and most delicious thanks to provide your metabolism a nudge towards a lower weight, reduced appetency and higher health. it'll conjointly build the remainder of the changes easier.

Adding a lot of protein to your diet can boost your metabolism and cut back your appetency, giving your metabolism a nudge and creating resultant changes abundant easier.

2. begin consumption a Healthy Breakfast, ideally With Eggs

The second step involves dynamical one in every of your daily meals... breakfast.

Most people are consumption cereal or one thing similar for breakfast, however that actualy is that the worst issue you'll be able to erode the beginning of the day.

Most breakfast cereals are loaded with refined carbs and sugar (even the healthy trying ones).

Eating these items for breakfast can spike your glucose, resulting in a crash many hours later... followed by cravings for one more high-carb meal (9).

Instead, eat eggs for breakfast.

Eggs are just about the proper food... they're high in macromolecule, healthy fats and contain a large amount of nutrients.

There are many studies showing that if you replace a grain-based breakfast (bagels) with eggs, it will assist you lose fat.

Eggs are best served with vegetables or a fruit... however you'll be able to have quality bacon with them if you wish.

If you can't eat eggs for a few reason, any high-protein, nutrient dense food can answer.

There extremely is not any valid excuse to not eat a healthy breakfast. Once you get this into a routine, getting ready an egg-based breakfast doesn't take over 5-10 minutes, at most. simply set your alarm a small amount earlier.

That being aforesaid, there's no have to be compelled to eat breakfast within the morning if you don't want it, simply ensure that your 1st meal of the day could be a healthy one. Eating a healthy, nutrient-dense breakfast with macromolecule and healthy fats is that the best thanks to begin the day.

3. Replace shitty Fats and Oils With sensible Fats and Oils

Simply substitution unhealthy fats and oils with healthier ones will have a significant impact on your health down the road.

Most people are consumption tons of seriously unhealthy fats... together with trans fats and refined vegetable oils.

Although trans fat consumption has gone down within the past few years and decades, it's still method too high.

To avoid trans fats, ensure you browse the label on something you eat. If it says "hydrogenated" or "partially hydrogenated" anyplace on the label, avoid it.

Refined vegetable oils are problematic. they need a distinct composition than alternative a lot of natural fats, being by artificial means high in omega-6 fatty acid fatty acids. This includes vegetable oil, vegetable oil, vegetable oil and several other others.

Without moving into the main points (you will examine them here), intense vegetable oils is also resulting in enlarged inflammation and aerophilous injury within the body, probably raising your risk of cardiopathy and cancer.

Instead of these nasty fats and oils, opt for fats that are largely saturated and/or monounsaturated. Grass-fed butter, oil, olive oil, avocado oil et al. Whole fruity are a superb supply of fat furthermore.

The comparatively easy act of substitution trans fats and high omega-6 fatty acid vegetable oils with healthy, ancient fats ought to cause some pretty spectacular health advantages and build your body perform higher.

4. take away Sugar-Sweetened Beverages and Fruit Juices From Your Diet

Sugar is unhealthy news... however sugar consumed in a very liquid kind is even worse.

Studies show that the brain willn't "register" liquid sugar calories within the same method because it does calories from alternative foods.

So you may drink many hundred calories of soda in someday (not uncommon), however your brain doesn't take them under consideration once it's attempting to regulate your energy

If you were to feature an entire food to your diet, you'd mechanically eat less of alternative foods instead. In alternative words, your brain would "compensate" for those additional calories.

That doesn't happen with liquid sugar calories. Your brain doesn't complete them, therefore you finish up taking in additional than you would like.

One study shows that intense one serving of sugar-sweetened beverages per day is coupled to a 60% enlarged risk of avoirdupois in kids.

Many alternative studies support this... sugar-sweetened beverages is also the foremost finished facet of the trendy diet.

Keep in mind that potable is simply as unhealthy. It contains identical quantity of sugar as a syrupy drinkable.

Sugar is also the one worst ingredient within the trendy diet, however intense it in a very liquid kind is even worse.

5. begin exercise... realize one thing that you just fancy and may keep on with

Exercise is one in every of the foremost necessary belongings you will do for each physical and psychological state, furthermore as sickness interference.

On its own, it's unlikely to guide to important weight loss.

However... it will facilitate improve your body composition. you'll not be losing weight, however you'll be losing some fat and gaining a small amount of muscle instead.

Exercise results in such a lot of advantages that it's on the far side the scope of this text to list all of them... however let's simply say that exercise is extremely protecting against just about any chronic, Western sickness.

It is conjointly implausibly helpful for mood, well-being and avoiding depression, that could be a quite common downside these days.

When it involves exercise, what you are doing specifically isn't that necessary. what's necessary is finding one thing that you just fancy doing and may keep on with within the long-standing time.

Although a mixture of vessel exercise and a few sort of resistance coaching is also the most effective, one thing as easy as walking conjointly has implausibly powerful health advantages.

If you've already done steps 1-4, the perform of your hormones ought to have improved and your energy levels enlarged, therefore beginning An exercise program might not be that arduous.

Work your high to performing some form of exercise a minimum of three times per week.

Exercise is simply as necessary as nutrition once it involves optimum health. It will improve each physical and psychological state, whereas being extremely protecting against latest, chronic diseases.

6. Replace Sugar, Refined Carbs and trendy Wheat With alternative Healthier Foods

Time to induce eliminate all the "bad" carbs.

Sugar and refined carbs are a number of the unhealthiest aspects of the trendy diet.

They're low in nutrients and fiber and contribute to gluttony, that brings with it a excessiveness of metabolic issues and diseases.

Wheat is in a very league of its own. trendy dwarf wheat, introduced around 1960, is low in nutrients compared to older types of wheat and is far worse for celiac patients and protein sensitive people than older types of wheat.

Instead of the "bad" carbs, opt for healthier carb sources instead. Vegetables, fruits, potatoes, sweet potatoes, healthier grains like rice, oats and quinoa, even legumes if you'll be able to tolerate them.

Whatever you are doing, simply get eliminate the sugar and processed carbs from your diet. Eat real food instead.

Sugar and refined carbs are a number of the foremost damaging aspects of the trendy diet. It's time to induce eliminate them and eat healthier carbs instead.

7. begin consumption Meat or Fish and lots of Vegetables for Dinner

Now it's time to remodel another one in every of your daily meals... dinner.

Replace no matter it's that you're consumption with a meal supported either meat or fish, at the side of lots of wholesome vegetables.

I realize that dinner is that the best meal to suit in lots of veggies.

If you fancy starches (like potatoes or rice) with dinner, then be at liberty to eat those too.

Definitely attempt to eat fatty fish a minimum of 1-2 times per week for all the super healthy Omega-3s. If you can't or won't eat fatty fish, then supplement with animal oil.

Start consumption a healthy dinner supported meat or fish, with lots of vegetables. attempt to eat fatty fish a minimum of 1-2 times per week.

8. Match Carb Intake to Your Metabolic Health and Activity Levels

Carbs are a extremely polemic nutrient.

Some assume the most important a part of our diet ought to be coming back from carbs, whereas others assume they're downright unhealthful.

As with most things, the reality is somewhere in between and depends greatly on the individual.

The optimum carb intake for anyone individual depends on several factors... together with metabolic health, activity levels, food culture and private preference.

Whereas somebody who is lean, healthy and lifts weights five times every week might perform well consumption tons of carbs, somebody who is overweight and doesn't exercise abundant can most likely do higher with a low-carb diet.

Although there's no scientific paper that explains specifically a way to match sugar intake to individual desires, I've in person found these pointers to be effective:

100–150 grams: those that are lean, healthy and physically active (some individuals might have even over this).

50–100 grams: those that are overweight and/or don't exercise abundant.

20–50 grams: those that have tons of weight to lose, or have metabolic issues like sort a pair of polygenic disorder. If weight loss is your goal, you'll be able to slowly add back in healthier carb sources after you reach your ideal weight.

Some individuals perform best consumption lots of carbohydrates. For others, low-carb diets have life saving advantages. It's necessary to match sugar intake to your individual desires and preferences.

9. lookout of Your mode... accenting Adequate Sleep and Reduced Stress Levels

Often unnoticed, sleep and stress levels will have a significant impact on your health.

Studies show that not obtaining enough sleep is powerfully coupled to several serious diseases, together with avoirdupois (34, 35).

Short sleep length may very well be one in every of the strongest risk issue for weight gain. it's coupled to a 55% enlarged risk of avoirdupois in adults and 89% in kids (36Trusted Source).

There are many ways to boost sleep... like sleeping in a very fully dark area, avoiding caffein within the afternoon and evening, furthermore as maintaining an identical sleep schedule.

Another major mode issue is chronic stress.

Excess stress raises your levels of the secretion adrenal cortical steroid, which might cause you to gain tons of fat within the abdomen and lift your risk of all kinds of health issues down the road (37, 38Trusted Source).

Unfortunately, stress may be arduous to wear down. several people are flooded with numerous duties and worries.

Meditation will facilitate with this, however if you're severely stressed all the time and can't realize some way to alter it on your own, then it's going to be an honest plan to hunt skilled facilitate.

Lifestyle factors like obtaining adequate sleep and avoiding chronic stress are implausibly necessary for optimum health, however usually unnoticed.

10. begin consumption Healthy Lunches and Snacks... currently every of Your Daily Meals ought to Be Healthy and wholesome

Now that you've already taken care of breakfast and dinner, it's time to maneuver on to lunches and snacks.

These meals tend to be the foremost problematic for tons of individuals, as a result of they're usually eaten far from home.

A good thanks to perpetually make sure you will eat one thing healthy for lunch is to cook an excessive quantity at dinner, therefore you'll be able to eat leftovers for lunch succeeding day.

But today, as a result of the planet is a lot of health acutely aware than ever before, "fast food" places that serve healthy food have started showing everywhere the place.

It might be an honest plan to jot down down an inventory of places that serve healthier foods, therefore you mostly have some choices accessible if you discover yourself hungry far from home.

Snacks are pretty straightforward... a chunk of fruit and one or two of fruity works well. many arduous cooked eggs, a bag of baby carrots... all of those are simply transportable.

Chances are that you just won't even want snacks at now, since avoiding sugar and processed carbs tends to cut back hunger and cause stable energy levels.

It's time to start out consumption healthy lunches and snacks each day. currently every of your meals ought to be healthy and wholesome. It will facilitate to arrange ahead and have an inventory of "fast food" places that serve healthy foods.

11. Cut Out All Processed Foods and begin specializing in Quality

Now it's time to travel fully real food based mostly.

You should already be 90% there, however if you've been hanging on to something that you just assume is also doing you hurt, now's the time to induce eliminate it.

Clear out your larder... throw away all soda, bread, cereals, flour, sugars, pastries and processed foods. Start specializing in quality ingredients... seek for quality sources of animal foods, opt for grass-fed if you'll be able to.

Eat quality manufacture and check out to avoid any food with artificial ingredients.

Remember... real food doesn't want an ingredients list, as a result of real food is that the ingredient.

It's time to clear your house of all unhealthy, artificial stuff. begin specializing in quality, unprocessed foods at each meal. seek for the healthiest sources of plants and animals.

12. attempt to a lifespan of Improvement

Turn health and nutrition into a hobby.

Subscribe to some blogs and check out to browse many health connected books annually.

Stay health acutely aware for the remainder of your life and you'll live longer, look higher and avoid most of the chronic diseases that individuals suffer from in maturity.

There's a fine line between thinking rigorously concerning what we tend to place into our bodies and obsessing over it or limiting it hazardously.

Whether our explicit issue is emotional consumption, binge consumption, disordered consumption or we tend to simply can't appear to induce a handle on the entire nutrition issue, we will all stand to find out many things from the individuals for whom healthy consumption simply comes simply. Here are many of the items they are doing otherwise.

1. individuals with a healthy relationship to food eat heedfully.

Our body has some pretty important intrinsic cues to inform once to eat -- and when to prevent consumption. however we're not perpetually listening. The follow of participating all of our senses to guide our consumption-related choices is named conscious eating for conscious consumption. conscious consumption will facilitate "acknowledge our response to food while not moving into judgement".

2. They swear by everything -- affirmative, everything -- sparsely.

The Essential Guide To Taking Care Of Your Mind And Body

Morality hooked up to food might stem from the very fact that some religions do have prohibitions once it involves food, he says. Take, as an example, however "some foods are delineated as sinfully delicious," he says.

"It isn't food that's sensible or unhealthy, it's our expertise," says dramatist. "And that's not judgement, it's categorizing." Recognizing foods and consumption things that you just realize pleasant will facilitate inform your future decisions, she says. individuals with a healthy relationship to food tell themselves, "'Eating could be a likelihood on behalf of me to nourish and nurture my being,'" she says, "as critical, 'I have to be compelled to eat this fashion or those foods.'"

3. however they recognize the temporal order should be right.

However, if you are doing decide you're within the mood for fries or dish or chocolate, says Abramson, fancy your choose at a time once you're not hungry for a full meal, therefore you don't make it. "If you're starving and so you're confronted with a favourite food, you'll consume tons a lot of of it," he says. "Let's say, if you have got it for sweet, you already had your meal, your tummy is full, you'll be able to extremely appreciate the sensations that chocolate provides."

4. They eat once they're physically hungry.

"Emotional consumption is often to assuage unpleasant arousal," says Abramson. sadly, stress and anxiety usually cause us to crave higher-calorie, fattier foods and "most people don't want further caloric intake," he says.

When we use food to do to assuage an feeling, he adds, we tend to mask what that feeling is attempting to show us, and instead replace it with regret or guilt for consumption no matter we tend to grabbed.

5. and that they stop consumption once they're well full.

Hunger and repletion each start up little and grow larger and louder, says dramatist. "Some people don't hear hunger or fullness till it's screaming in our ears," she says. however being more tuned-in whereas consumption will facilitate us "hear" higher furthermore. "Mindfulness is locution, 'I'm attending to listen tougher to my hunger and listen to it once it's not yelling at me, and I'm attending to listen tougher to my fullness therefore it's not yelling at me [either].'" each hunger and fullness modification once each bite, therefore listening in will assist you realize the extent of fullness wherever it's comfy for you to prevent consumption, she says.

6. They eat breakfast.

Regular breakfast eaters have a lot of energy, higher reminiscences and lower sterol. They conjointly feel healthier overall and are usually throw than their peers that don't eat a morning meal. "Starting your day with a healthy, balanced breakfast with proteins, fats and carbs and not high in sugar is that the key to healthy consumption," says Marjorie Nolan plant scientist, MS, RD, CDN, a advocator for the Academy of Nutrition & bioscience and therefore the author of Overcoming Binge consumption For Dummies.

7. They don't keep problematic foods within the house.

Once you recognize your specific patterns of emotional consumption, says Abramson, you'll be able to take little steps to send them. One strategy he recommends is not any longer keeping a very tempting food within the house, therefore you'd have to be compelled to leave home once dinner to induce a style. If, as an example, you actually love frozen dessert, "rather than having it sitting within the deep freezer occupation your name," he says, a handful of times every week, withdraw for frozen dessert.

8. They don't sit down with the entire bag.

Hitting up your native frozen dessert search conjointly has the good thing about providing your treat in a very single serving size. "If you have got a cup or a cone you recognize once you're finished, as critical sitting there having one containerful once another" straight out of the carton, says Abramson. shopping for single-serving packages of your favorite chips or cookies may also facilitate, he says, as will merely serving yourself in a very cup or bowl instead of sitting down with an entire family-size bag of chips.

9. They recognize the distinction between a snack and a treat.

Letting yourself get too hungry could be a instruction for gluttony -- particularly those foods you most wish to stay to smaller parts. Snacking could be a good thanks to ensure you're not ravenous return suppertime. however snack alternative is crucial to each keeping you full and keeping your healthy consumption plans not off course, says Abramson. "A treat is only for enjoyment, whereas a snack are some things you eat between meals to ward off hunger," he says. "Nuts or fruit or cheese may be an honest snack," he says, however chocolate? A treat.

10. they offer themselves permission to fancy consumption.

These tips aren't plausible if we tend to don't build time to price our relationships with food. "So persistently we tend to forget to require the time to eat, and consumption will take time," says dramatist.

She suggests trying ahead at your day and ensuring you have got enough time sculptured bent eat, instead of going to scarf one thing down within the 3 minutes you have got between afternoon conferences. "We build it 3 minutes, which might feed you, however will it nourish you?" she asks. And it's not concerning feeling guilty for missing one thing else by creating time to eat, she says. It's concerning really basic cognitive process we tend to are "worth sitting down and consumption food."

11. They don't "make up" for a meal.

When we realize ourselves feeling guilty a few food alternative, "there's this instinct to create up for it by either overdoing it at the athletic facility or being terribly restrictive at succeeding meal," says plant scientist. Instead, she suggests thinking of this method as a a lot of refined "balancing out". individuals with healthy relationships to food can have a lighter meal later within the day if they attempt to indulge at brunch, as an example, however they won't limit that later meal most in order that they find yourself binging later as a result of they've created themselves too hungry. "You will balance out slowly over the course of every week, however you can't form up among identical day," says plant scientist.

12. They don't eat to check the dimensions shift.

Ideally, we'd all eat what makes us feel sensible, says Cohn. We'd choose the foods that gave us energy to fuel our daily activity, and we'd avoid foods that, say, gave us stomach upset, despite however sensible they tasted, instead of restructuring our consumption plans to create the quantity on the dimensions modification.

13. They're not frightened of feeling hungry.

One of the foremost restrictive patterns of thought that plant scientist sees among purchasers could be a concern of consumption an excessive amount of and consequently gaining weight. "People who have a way of what their body desires and eat heedfully and intuitively once they will, they're not as frightened of their hunger," she says. "What's there to be afraid of? If you get hungry, you simply eat something!"

Some things can't be controlled (your age, case history of diseases, gender). however others will. and people things aren't a large surprise — you already understand to not smoke, drink an excessive amount of, or eat crappily.

It's fascinating, though, however all of the main diseases are caused by constant things: smoking, diet, exercise, alcohol and stress.

Below I'll list the highest habits you'll amendment, and a straightforward methodology for dynamical them.

The Habits of Healthy Living

1. Stop smoking. this can be far and away the foremost vital habit, because it affects virtually each single one amongst the leading causes of death. It's conjointly the toughest of those habits to vary. It's not the least bit not possible — I quit six years past next month (read my tips).

2. change state (if you're overweight). this can be not precisely a habit — the most effective habit to create to change state is to eat less. Or eat a lot of of things that don't have tons of calories, like fruits and veggies. Being overweight is simply below smoking the worst risk issue for several diseases.

3. Exercise. You don't would like ME to inform you to exercise, however hear this: lack of exercise may be a major risk issue for cardiovascular disease, stroke, colon & body part cancers, diabetes, carcinoma, high pressure and high steroid alcohol. If you don't exercise, you're simply asking to urge a serious unwellness. It's virtually a magic pill: do a touch of exercise a day, and you get healthy. You don't would like a lot of — begin with five minutes on a daily basis within the morning.

4. Drink solely carefully. serious drinking is one amongst the worst risk factors for several diseases. That's quite a pair of drinks of alcohol on a daily basis for men, and quite one drink for ladies. A glass of vino may be a sensible factor, however too several and you're greatly increasing your risk of unwellness.

5. Cut out red & processed meats. consumption red meats, and processed meats like sausages, bacon, canned meats so on, may be a risk issue for colon/rectal cancer, abdomen cancer, and high steroid alcohol, that successively may be a leading risk issue for coronary cardiovascular disease and stroke. whereas this won't sit well with many folks, the overwhelming mass of analysis supports this. i like to recommend going feeder.

6. Eat fruits & veggies. this can be obvious, however it's superb however few veggies the general public eat. consumption fruits and veggies reduces your risk of many leading diseases, and it's one amongst the best habits to create. Eat a dish (without serious dressings, bacon or alternative meats, croutons or cheese), add green groceriess to soups or veggie chili, cook up veggies as a healthy entremots with dinner or lunch. Eat fruits with breakfast and as snacks.

7. scale back salt, and saturated/trans fats. Salt and saturated or trans fats are in numerous processed or ready foods, and that they increase risks of high pressure and high steroid alcohol, that increase risk for cardiovascular disease and stroke. Despite what the photographer worth

Foundation and others on the web tell you, saturated fat isn't healthy — browse the sources. Note that this isn't an argument within the health profession, however the "harmlessness" of saturated fats is perpetuated by the diary and meat industries, and lay writers like metropolis Taube. Cook your own healthy meals rather than consumption out or eating ready foods.

8. scale back stress. Stress may be a risk issue for cardiovascular disease and high pressure, that is itself a risk issue for stroke. change your workday in order that you're not excessively stressed, and exercise to alleviate stress.

Here's a way to amendment these habits:
Change only 1 habit at a time. It doesn't matter that habit you select. simply select one. You'll need to try to to quite one, but don't.
Create positive habits you relish. browse the last word once more — if you relish it, the habit amendment are going to be straightforward. Replace smoking with positive habits you relish that fulfill the wants that smoking currently fulfills (stress reduction, social lubrication, tedium relief, etc.). Replace red meats with healthy foods you relish.

Start as tiny as attainable. simply do five minutes the primary week, and take a look at to be consistent as attainable. Then do ten minutes. chickenfeed is far and away the foremost effective methodology I've used for dynamical habits. Slow amendment lasts.

Make it social. realize a partner or cluster to vary the habit with you, therefore you're a lot of doubtless to stay with it.

These work. I've done them over and over, and each time I follow these principles, I've modified a habit.

Healthy living isn't not possible, or maybe particularly troublesome. It's simply slower to return by than the general public look after.

Healthy habits can avoid diseases

One of the most effective ways that to keep up your health is by taking care of yourself. If you would like to measure a healthy life style and revel in your maturity while not being injected with many totally different forms of shots, then amendment your daily life style as a result of even the best very little healthy modification will cause nice edges.

Though it's troublesome to place health and fitness as a prime priority during this routine day and age, it's best to begin with baby steps can sure peak your health enormously.

Healthy Habit to Avoid unwellness # 1: Wash your hands usually

Not laundry hands before a meal is one amongst the quickest means you'll fall sick. throughout our daily chores, we tend to tend to the touch many things at a time knowing and inadvertently. because of this daily mechanism, germs will get simply transported from our hands to our mouth. Hence, continually instill the habit of laundry hands often to stay health issues at a hands distance.

Healthy Habit to Avoid unwellness # 2: Stop nose choosing

This habit of dig gold' is one amongst the worst health habits. choosing your nose perpetually will cause and unfold varied infections like cold and influenza since cold virus is passed into your body through the secretion. once touching many things then taking constant finger into your nose, can make sure that you land at the doctor's clinic. Hence, stop this awkward habit of onanism sticky substance from your nose.

Healthy Habit to Avoid unwellness # 3: Stretching is vital

Make stretching an area of your daily activities. Since we tend to pay most of our time ina workplace and infront of the pc, our muscles tend to become stiff and contracted . This stiffness will increase the chance of injuries and sever pains. To avoid these injuries, ensure to often pratice stretching each morning.

Healthy Habit to Avoid unwellness # 4: Breathe the proper means

we should always breathe from our diaphragm rather than respiratory from our chest. this alteration within the respiratory pattern will facilitate to maximise the element intake and can conjointly make sure that you keep calm. amendment your respiratory vogue to enhance the means your body functions and blood circulation.

Healthy Habit to Avoid unwellness # 5:Eat a healthy breakfast

Always ensure that you simply eat a healthy breakfast each morning. Breakfast is that the most vital meal of the day and a consumption a healthy breakfast within the morning can assist you to avoid snacking throughout the remainder of the day. Result? you'll stop upset stomach that is caused because of digestion downside and weight gain.

Healthy Habit to Avoid unwellness # 6: Bathing is sweet

Make sure you cleanse yourself totally with an honest refreshing shower gel or soap. an honest shower is critical to get rid of dirt and odor from your body and bathing conjointly helps you to revitalize. build your shower time a spoil time, by improvement every a part of your body totally to stop infection and foul odor.

Healthy Habit to Avoid unwellness # 7: Cut your nails often

Long nails won't solely build acting your daily tasks troublesome however it may also act as a bunch for infections and germs. after you bit many things, there's a large possibilities of the germs obtaining stuck into your nails – says Dr. Sunesara. These germs will pass to your mouth, after you nibble your food.

Healthy Habit to Avoid unwellness # 8: Avoid sharing personal things

Sharing personal things like razors, toothbrush and nail clips etc. will cause germ transfer. Keep your personal things only for you. ne'er share any item even together with your relations.

Healthy Habit to Avoid unwellness # 9: continually apply sunblock

Make a habit of applying an honest sunblock on your skin, whenever you venture out.This habit can keep varied skin issues like carcinoma and malignant melanoma cornered. Besides, it'll conjointly decrease skin harm and provides you a younger wanting skin for a protracted time.

Healthy Habit to Avoid unwellness # 10: Say no to sweet things

Sugary things are as toxicant as alcohol and cigarettes. Excess presence of sugar in your body, will have sever negative effects on your weight and skin. Avoid sweet things and sweet sodas to stay polygenic disease and alternative chronic diseases cornered.

Healthy Habit to Avoid unwellness # 11: Sweat it out

Give a break to your inactive life by adding a touch exercise to that. exertion often for half-hour have endless edges because it helps to keep up healthy weight, decreases tension and boosts your energy levels and mood. begin exertion keep healthy and to avoid varied vas diseases.

Healthy Habit to Avoid unwellness # 12: sensible sleep

Never compromise on your sleeping hours. an honest night's sleep for eight hours is incredibly vital to stop varied sleep disorders. Thus, continually maintain a correct schedule and proper sleeping pattern. select a snug bed and ne'er eat a significant meal late in the dead of night.

Healthy Habit to Avoid unwellness # 13: Stop worrying
The best factor favour you'll do to yourself is by avoiding stress like plague. Stress is that the reason behind varied health issues like depression, sleep disorder and heart disorder. Dr. Sunesara says – whenever stressed, apply respiratory exercise and relax yourself.

Healthy Habit to Avoid unwellness # 14: Monitor your monitor time
Reduce your monitor time, to avoid negative impact on your eyes and psychological state – says Dr. Sunesara. If your work depends on the usage of monitors then shield yourself by victimization sensible try of eye protection glasses and regulate the means you sit. Besides, ensure you avoid watching any reasonably a monitor before bed time to urge an honest nights sleep.

Healthy Habit to Avoid unwellness # 15: Drink millions of water

Drink a minimum of 8-10 glasses of water a day, betting on your physical activity. sufficient intake of water is incredibly essential to flush out toxins from your body and to rejuvenate your cells. If you are doing not drink enough water, you'll finish dehydrated yourself and therefore, exhausted.

Healthy Habit to Avoid unwellness # 16: Say no to food

Fast food is made in trans fat, sugar, spices and artificial preservatives. perpetually intense food can expand your area and cause serious health issues within the long haul like high steroid alcohol, polygenic disease and heart issues. Since sustenance is made in unhealthy fat, it raises the unhealthy steroid alcohol within the body and results in the hardening of the arteries, which might more cause plaque deposits. Hence, switch to a healthier diet and shield yourself from weight gain and alternative serious successfulness issues.

Healthy Habit to Avoid unwellness # 17: Quit smoking

Smoking even one coffin nail on a daily basis, will cause blood clots, {which may|which will} stop swift flow of the blood and therefore can cause plaque to develop in your arteries and blood vessels. Besides, you'll conjointly harm the lifetime of the nonsmoker WHO lives with you.

Healthy Habit to Avoid unwellness # 18: keep safe whereas having sex

Sex may be a enjoyable act and if you act foolish you'll land in serious health issues. continually use a prophylactic device whereas having sex to stop sexually transmitted diseases and avoid unwanted physiological state. Besides, don't be a Casanova, follow one partner for your sexual pleasures.

Healthy Habit to Avoid unwellness # 19: Respect your body and yourself

Your body is your host, learn to respect it. settle for each flaw and weaknes and learn to measure with it. If you would like to remain pleased with physiological condition and high confidence then love your body the means it's.

Healthy Habit to Avoid unwellness # 20: begin enamored vegetables

The first habit to feature in your consumption collection is to add every type of vegetables in your diet. The health edges of consumption vegetables are varied. Vegetables are loaded with fiber, essential vitamins and varied nutrients that promote physiological condition in each means.

A habit is outlined within the Merriam-Webster wordbook as a "usual means of behaving: one thing that someone will usually in a very regular and perennial way." The key word during this definition is "repeated".

Indeed, no matter activities you are doing to keep up your health, it's solely through repetition that you simply can deliver the goods your goals. Running a half-marathon once a year can at the best offer you with a lift of endorphins or at the worst, an injury. On the opposite hand, half-hour of walking or cardiopulmonary exercise many times per week, year-round, can do miracles for your quality of life and health.

Here are twenty healthy daily habits which will assist you improve your physical and mental well-being. Ideally, decide one then wait till it's totally integrated into your daily routine before choosing another!

Walking

Whenever you'll. to travel to the foodstuff or the workplace, to urge some recent air throughout your lunch break or to visit whereas in a very new town. Walk. The minimum range of steps you must be taking a day is ten,000. it would seem to be tons, however each minute counts and gets you nearer to your goal. think about it as a game!

Stand up on an everyday basis

Prolonged inactivity may be a downside that's as current as a general lack of exercise. Staying sitting throughout hours at a time compromises the body's ability to consume fats and sugars, which might cause many health issues. Thankfully, there's a straightforward solution: get up as usually as attainable. Head to your colleague's workplace, get up once you're on the phone, or use the steps. each reason may be a sensible one to urge active every day!

Play outside

Getting some recent air a day is one amongst the best and most pleasant ways that of rising your health. Recent studies have even shown the numerous health edges of natural daylight. [1] what is more, disbursement time outside may be a great way to manage your stress. [2]

Straighten your posture

You should set regular reminders (alarms or notes) to straighten your posture! Bring your neck and hips into a neutral position, then pull your shoulder blades back and stick your chest out. an honest posture helps each muscle add AN best means and reduces pressure on your joints. within the long haul, you'll scale back your risk of obtaining back aches and within the short run, you'll feel a lot of assured, energized, and you'll be able to breathe higher.

Use your muscles

Whether to counter muscle loss related to aging, to stop osteoporosis or back aches, or to easily build any activity easier, it's in your best interest to use your muscles as usually as attainable. Take the steps, prolong a hike, do some push ups, check in for a yoga category. These are solely a number of ways that of exertion your muscles a day.

Stretch

You don't need to stretch for AN hour, you'll merely improve your flexibility by moving your body in numerous ways that a number of minutes a day. By adding a number of stretches to your daily routine, you'll increase your joint flexibility, which can scale back your risk of injury. Moreover, you'll get an immediate boost of energy because of the inflow of ventilated blood sent to your muscles and brain.

Move together with your friends

This is a two-in-one: it's fun and motivating! indeed, motivating others is one amongst the best ways that to stay yourself impelled. And by exertion together with your friends, you'll associate being active with fun and you'll need to try to to it regularly!

CHAPTER 9:

Food

Eat in sensible company

Set your screens aside and pay your time connecting with real humans. Not solely may be a voice communication a good thanks to reinforce your social bonds, it'll cause you to eat a lot of slowly. You'll set your fork down after you feel full, however not too full.

Fill half of your plate with fruits and vegetables

Many people understand this tip, however few people follow it. after you arrange your menu, add millions of salads, stews, soups, raw vegetables, gratins, purees, sautés, recent fruit, smoothies, and compotes. Fruits and veggies are jam-choked with nutrients, low in calories, and cheap. the best ingredients to a healthy diet!

Pay attention to after you feel hungry and full

How much do you have to eat each day? the solution to the current question will vary greatly and depends on your weight, gender, age, and physical activity level. That being aforesaid, an honest thanks to guarantee you're consumption enough is to listen to your hunger signals. once your abdomen growls, eat. after you feel full, stop. even though your plate isn't empty. even though somebody offers you second helpings.

Add selection to your diet

By adding selection to your menu, you'll make sure you have gotten a variety of distinctive edges from a large choice of ingredients. for example, rather than your regular morning toast, strive AN nightlong oatmeal or add otherwise colored vegetables to your cart.

Breakfast > lunch > dinner

Because you wish to focus and keep energized throughout the daytime, you must eat a filling breakfast, a medium-sized lunch, and a lightweight dinner. You'll visit bed feeling lighter and you'll get up feeling peckish. that is what you wish to begin everywhere again!

Drink lots of water

Water is crucial for staying hydrous and avoiding headaches, fatigue, and issues focusing. Keep a reusable bottle to be had and continually place it seeable to cue you to drink often. Tea, herbal tea, and nonsweet occasional are sensible choices.

Pack your lunch

Preparing your own lunch and snacks for the workplace, school, or travels may be a great way to eat the go. Not solely can you save cash, you'll avoid excess metal, sugar, fat, and chemical preservatives in meals at sustenance restaurants.

Take the time to cook

By cooking, we tend to mean taking your time throughout the week to arrange a number of easy, tasty dishes that may prevent time on busy days. It solely takes 2 hours to cook twelve muffins, slice a melon and vegetables, marinade bean curd, and cook quinoa.

Putting away your smartphone may appear like a huge challenge. however being connected 24/7 will have negative facet effects on your memory, creativity, and productivity. Disconnect a minimum of one hour a day and provides your brain a well-deserved break!

Breathe

Take your time to require deep breaths. With everything that's happening around you, you may solely be taking short, shallow breaths. disbursement a number of moments respiratory deeply will calm your mind and supply physical edges, like lowering your pressure and rate. It may also assist you manage your stress.

Enjoy a micro-vacation

Every day? If you can! It solely takes half AN hour. A micro-vacation merely suggests that an instant in your day after you will rest and relax. Lie back and stare off into the gap.

Let your brain wander. You'll be shocked at however helpful this may be for your creative thinking and energy levels!

Sleep

Sleep, a bit like exercise and a healthy diet, is one amongst the pillars of excellent health. obtaining enough sleep (between seven and eight hours each night) on an everyday basis can have a positive impact on your mood, memory, longevity, also as your psychological feature and physical performance.

Smile

This is a straightforward habit to adopt and can greatly impact your mood. merely raising the corners of your mouth produces endorphins, providing instant happiness!

In conclusion, one amongst the benefits of adopting healthy life style habits is that it's attainable to keep up them forever. This isn't always attainable with extreme solutions that usually turn out to be a furor. By that specialize in healthy life style habits, you'll guarantee your success is long -lasting!

Morning Habits That assist you change state

No matter what your weight loss goals are, losing weight will feel not possible sometimes.

However, shedding a number of pounds doesn't need to involve an entire overhaul of your current diet and life style. In fact, creating a number of tiny changes to your morning routine will assist you change state and keep it off.

1. Eat a High-Protein Breakfast

There's an honest reason breakfast is taken into account the foremost vital meal of the day.

What you eat for breakfast will set the course for your entire day. It determines if you'll feel full and glad till lunch, or if you'll be heading to the coin machine before your mid-morning snack.

Eating a high-protein breakfast might facilitate cut cravings and aid in weight loss.

In one study in twenty adolescent women, consumption a high-protein breakfast reduced post-meal cravings a lot of effectively than a normal-protein breakfast.

Another tiny study showed that consumption a high-protein breakfast was related to less fat gain and reduced daily intake and hunger, compared to a normal-protein breakfast.

Protein may additionally aid weight loss by decreasing levels of hormone, the "hunger hormone" that's answerable for increasing craving.

In fact, one study in fifteen men found that a high-protein breakfast suppressed hormone secretion a lot of effectively than a high-carb breakfast.

To help get your break day to an honest begin, think about supermolecule sources like eggs, Greek yoghourt, pot cheese, loco and chia seeds.

Studies show that a high-protein breakfast might aid weight loss by reducing cravings, craving and hormone secretion.

2. Drink lots of Water

Starting your morning with a glass or 2 of water is a straightforward thanks to enhance weight loss.

Water will facilitate increase your energy expenditure, or the amount of calories your body burns, for a minimum of hour.

In one tiny study, drinking sixteen.9 fluid ounces (500 ml) of water diode to a 30% increase in rate, on the average.

Another study found that overweight ladies WHO increased their water intake to over thirty four ounces (one liter) per day lost an additional 4.4 pounds (2 kg) over one year, while not creating the other changes in their diet or exercise routine.

What's a lot of, potable might scale back craving and food intake in some people.

One study in twenty four older adults showed that drinking sixteen.9 fluid ounces (500 ml) of water reduced the amount of calories consumed at breakfast by 13%.

In fact, most studies on the subject have shown that drinking 34–68 ounces (1–2 liters) of water per day will aid in weight loss.

Starting your morning with water and staying well hydrous throughout the day may be a good way to spice up weight loss with stripped-down effort.

Increasing your water intake has been related to a rise in weight loss and energy expenditure, also as a decrease in craving and food intake.

3. Weigh Yourself

Stepping on the dimensions and deliberation yourself every morning is an efficient methodology to extend motivation and improve self-control.

Several studies have associated deliberation yourself daily with bigger weight loss.

For instance, a study in forty seven individuals found that those that weighed themselves daily lost concerning thirteen pounds (6 kg) a lot of over six months than those who weighed themselves less usually.

Another study reportable that adults WHO weighed themselves daily lost a mean of nine.7 pounds (4.4 kg) over a biennial amount, whereas those that weighed themselves once a month gained four.6 pounds (2.1 kg).

Weighing yourself each morning may also facilitate foster healthy habits and behaviors that will promote weight loss.

In one massive study, frequent self-weighing was related to improved restraint. what is more, those that stopped deliberation themselves often were a lot of doubtless to report increased calorie intake and decreased self-discipline.

For best results, weigh yourself right after you get up. Do therefore once victimization the lavatory and before you eat or drink something.

Additionally, bear in mind that your weight may fluctuate daily and may be influenced by a range of things. specialize in the massive image and appearance for overall weight loss trends, instead of obtaining fixated on tiny daily changes.

Studies have found that daily self-weighing is also related to a lot of weight loss and increased restraint.

4. Get Some Sun

Opening the curtains to let in some daylight or disbursement a number of further minutes outside every morning will facilitate kickstart your weight loss.

One tiny study found that exposure to even moderate levels of sunshine at sure times of the day will have an influence on weight.

Moreover, AN animal study found that exposure to actinic ray helped suppress weight gain in mice fed a high-fat diet.

Exposure to daylight is additionally the most effective thanks to meet your ergocalciferol wants. Some studies have found that meeting your ergocalciferol necessities will aid in weight loss and even stop weight gain.

In one study, 218 overweight and rotund ladies took either ergocalciferol supplements or a placebo for one year. At the top of the study, those that met their ergocalciferol demand lost a mean of seven pounds (3.2 kg) quite those with inadequate ergocalciferol blood levels.

Another study followed four,659 older ladies for four years and located that higher levels of ergocalciferol were joined to less weight gain.

The amount of sun exposure you wish will vary supported your skin kind, the season and your location. However, holding in some daylight or sitting outside for 10–15 minutes every morning might have a helpful impact on weight loss.

Sun exposure might have AN influence on weight. daylight may also assist you meet your ergocalciferol wants, which can facilitate increase weight loss and forestall weight gain.

5. apply attentiveness

Mindfulness may be a apply that involves totally that specialize in the current moment and transferral awareness to your thoughts and feelings.

The apply has been shown to boost weight loss and promote healthy consumption habits.

For example, AN analysis of nineteen studies found that mindfulness-based interventions increased weight loss and reduced obesity-related consumption behaviors.

Another review had similar findings, noting that attentiveness coaching resulted in vital weight loss in 68% of the studies reviewed.

Practicing attentiveness is straightforward. to urge started, strive disbursement 5 minutes every morning sitting well in a very calm area and connecting together with your senses.

Some studies have found that attentiveness will increase weight loss and promote healthy consumption behaviors.

6. Squeeze in Some Exercise

Getting in some physical activity very first thing within the morning will facilitate boost weight loss.

One study in fifty overweight ladies measured the results of cardiopulmonary exercise at totally different times of the day.

While there wasn't a lot of distinction noted in specific food cravings between those that exercised within the morning versus the afternoon, figuring out within the morning was related to the next level of satiation.

Exercising within the morning may additionally facilitate keep blood glucose levels steady throughout the day. Low blood glucose may end up in several negative symptoms, as well as excessive hunger.

One study in thirty five individuals with kind one polygenic disease showed that figuring out within the morning was related to improved blood glucose management.

However, these studies targeted on terribly specific populations ANd show an association, instead of deed. a lot of analysis on the results of morning exercise within the general population is required.

Some studies have found that exertion within the morning is also related to increased satiation and improved blood glucose management.

7. Pack Your Lunch

Making the trouble to arrange and pack your lunch prior time is a straightforward thanks to build higher food decisions and increase weight loss.

A large study as well as forty,554 individuals found that meal coming up with was related to higher diet quality, a lot of diet selection and a lower risk of fleshiness.

Another study found that consumption home-cooked meals a lot of often was related to improved diet quality and a decreased risk of excess body fat.

In fact, those that Ate home-cooked meals a minimum of 5 times per week were 28% less doubtless to be overweight than those who solely ate home-cooked meals 3 times or less per week.

Try setting aside a number of hours one night per week to arrange and prepare your meals in order that within the morning you'll simply grab your lunch and go.

Studies show that meal coming up with and consumption home-cooked meals are related to improved diet quality and a lower risk of fleshiness.

8. Sleep Longer

Going to bed a touch earlier or setting your timer later to squeeze in some further sleep might facilitate increase weight loss.

Several studies have found that sleep deprivation is also related to AN increased craving.

One tiny study found that sleep restriction increased hunger and cravings, particularly for high-carb, high-calorie foods.

Lack of sleep has conjointly been joined to a rise in calorie intake.

In one study, twelve participants consumed a mean of 559 a lot of calories once obtaining simply four hours of sleep, compared to after they got a full eight hours.

Establishing a healthy sleep schedule may be a important part of weight loss, along side consumption well and exertion. to maximise your results, aim for a minimum of eight hours of sleep per night.

Studies show that sleep deprivation might increase craving and cravings, also as calorie intake.

9. Switch up Your Commute

While driving is also one amongst the foremost convenient ways that to urge to figure, it's going to not be therefore nice for your area.

Research shows that walking, biking or by using public transportation is also tied to a lower weight and reduced risk of weight gain.

One study followed 822 individuals over four years and located that those that commuted by automotive attended gain a lot of weight than non-car commuters.

Similarly, a study as well as fifteen,777 individuals showed that using public transportation or active ways of transport, like walking or biking, was related to a considerably lower body mass index and body fat proportion, compared to using non-public transportation.

Changing up your commute even a number of times per week is also a straightforward thanks to build weight loss.

Walking, biking and using public transportation have all been related to less weight gain and lower weight and body fat, compared to driving to figure.

10. begin trailing Your Intake

Keeping a food diary to trace what you eat is an efficient thanks to facilitate boost weight loss and keep yourself responsible.

One study half-tracked weight loss in 123 individuals for one year and located that finishing a food journal was related to a bigger quantity of weight loss.

Another study showed that participants who often used a trailing system to self-monitor their diet and exercise lost a lot of weight than those that failed to regularly use the tracking system.

Similarly, a study of 220 rotund ladies found that the frequent and consistent use of a self-monitoring tool helped improve long-run weight management.

Try using AN app or maybe simply a pen and paper to record what you eat and drink, beginning together with your initial meal of the day.

Studies have found that employing a food diary to trace your intake will facilitate increase weight loss.

Making a number of tiny changes to your morning habits is a straightforward and effective thanks to increase weight loss.

Practicing healthy behaviors within the morning may also get your day started on the proper foot and set you up for fulfillment.

For best results, ensure you mix these morning habits with a all-around diet and healthy life style.

Have a transparent goal. It ought to be one that anyone within the world will live and perceive.

2. Drink tea. analysis suggests that those that drink tea – black, inexperienced or white, as long as it's from real tea versus tea – have lower BMIs and fewer body fat than those that don't consume tea.

3. Eat cayenne pepper. A study printed within the British Journal of Nutrition showed that in comparison to placebo, chemical irritant – the active ingredient in cayenne – increased fat burning.

4. Decrease/eliminate processed carbs. they are doing nothing for you outside of making a favourable setting for gaining fat.

5. Eat a lot of veggies. They fill you up, while not providing several kilojoules. simply avoid the high-kilojoule dressings.

6. Eat a lot of fruit. nobody ever gained weight from consumption a lot of fruit. which includes the supposed "high sugar" fruits like bananas and melons.

7. elevate weights. serious weights. Build a lot of muscle, burn a lot of kilojoules.

8. prevent rest time between sets. this may keep your rate elevated, inflicting a rise in kilojoules burned.

9. Do intervals. Study once study after study continues to indicate intervals are more practical and time economical than longer activity performed at a lower intensity.

10. Eat a lot of supermolecule. commutation refined carbohydrates with lean supermolecule won't solely facilitate satiate you, however also will increase your metabolism – through one thing referred to as the thermal impact of food.

11. Eat supermolecule a lot of often. It's vital to conjointly time your intake so you're consumption supermolecule often throughout the day – not simply in one payment, like most do at dinner. each meal and snack ought to embrace some supermolecule.

12. Supplement with animal oil. A study printed in Lipids fed mice diets increased epa and DHA – a.k.a. fish oil. The researchers learnt that the mice fed diets higher in polyunsaturated fatty acid fats had considerably less accumulation of body fat. alternative studies have shown similar results.

13. Do full body exercises. Think: Squats, deadlifts, chin-ups and pushups. You'll get a lot of bang for your buck out of every exertion.

14. Cycle your carb intake supported your activity level. Sure, carbs are vital. however on the times you don't calculate, you merely don't would like as several compared to the times you exercise exhausting. Rule of thumb: The a lot of active you're, the a lot of carbs you'll eat, and the other way around.

15. begin your meals with a dish. dish can offer some bulk to assist fill you up – in order that you eat less kilojoules overall.

16. Don't forget the fibre. think about fibre sort of a sponge; it absorbs water and causes you to feel full.

17. Drink water. prof Dr Brenda Davy and her team from Virginia school University found that giving individuals 2 cups of water before every meal resulted in bigger weight loss once twelve weeks. The reason? It helps fill you up.

18. Add beans to your salads. It's a pleasant thanks to add some further fibre, supermolecule and healthy carbs.

19. Replace one meal on a daily basis with an oversized dish and lean supermolecule. this can be a straightforward thanks to instantly improve your diet.

20. Keep a food journal. There's no higher thanks to track what you're putting in place your mouth.

21. Watch your parts. Avoid the buffet line and ne'er supersize. Instead ensure you're following what the nutrition label recommends for a serving.

22. Switch to kilojoule-free drinks. All kilojoules count, whether or not they're liquid or solid. therefore unless it's milk, elect tea or water. Or one thing i used to be introduced to within the Netherlands – massive bunches of mint, lemon and predicament.

23. Weigh yourself. Studies show daily weigh-ins facilitate enhance weight loss efforts. Don't live and die by the amount. And, of course, a scale doesn't decipher between fat

and lean body mass, however it will still be of profit to stay things "in check".

24. Eat whole eggs. Daily. A study printed a few years past showed that those that Ate whole eggs versus a beigel for breakfast ate less at future meal. the same study showed consumption whole eggs will increase high-density lipoprotein steroid alcohol.

25. Eat breakfast. A review printed within the yankee Journal of Clinical Nutrition showed that those that eat breakfast are a lot of booming with long-run weight maintenance. alternative analysis has shown constant for weight loss. Grab hardboiled eggs, disorganised eggs, Greek food, a bit of fruit and few loco, or build a smoothie. It doesn't need to be fancy.

26. Eat the majority of your meals within the A.M. Then eat more and more less throughout the day. A study printed within the Journal of Nutrition showed that consumption most of your kilojoules earlier in the day completely influences weight changes.

27. To burn a lot of kilojoules, keep upright. this suggests not sitting before of a pc, TV, phone, etc., all day long. Stand and you'll burn a lot of and be more productive.

28. Use the steps. That's right: Skip the escalator and elevator. This won't build or break success, however each

little helps.

29. Eat low-energy, dense foods. These are foods that are high in water and lower in calories, like fruit, veggies, soups and salads. Studies at Penn State University have shown that the inclusion of those foods helps people eat less total kilojoules overall.

30. Don't grocery search hungry. If you do, you'll obtain everything within the aisle – rather than sticking out to your list. And most of the time, the foods you get once hungry can the types that sabotage your weight-loss efforts.

31. Replace facet dishes with steamed veggies. Restaurants can usually permit you to substitute the fries or chips with steamed veggies. All you've got to try to to is raise.

32. Bake, don't fry. It's pretty easy extremely. Ditch the pans and switch thereon kitchen appliance.

33. Use the fat-burner in your backyard: Your grill. And as South Africans we tend to love an honest braai. simply skip the staff of life and select a tasty dish as a facet instead.

34. Order dressing on the facet. however here's the larger secret: Dip your fork in dressing, then within the dish. this protects a lot a lot of dressing than if one was to order it on the facet, then pour the complete cup on the dish anyway. Fewer kilojoules equal less weight.

35. within the airport: Carry your bags, don't roll it. Again, not a deal breaker in terms of success – simply otherwise to extend energy expenditure.

36. Skip the "Venti lattes" and elect plain occasional. (Or higher nonetheless, tea.) Those extra-large "designer" coffees will pack a belly-inflating a pair of 000 or a lot of kilojoules per serving!

37. Embrace oats. Plain oatmeal can facilitate fill you up quite the high sugar breakfast counterparts. Moreover, one serving provides tons less kilojoules than the sugary alternatives.

38. Fidget. A study printed within the journal Science showed that those that fidgeted a lot of usually – as an example, modified their posture often – weighed but those that didn't. This further movement was termed NEAT (non-exercise activity thermogenesis).

39. Laugh usually. A study bestowed on fleshiness found those that laughed exhausting for roughly ten to fifteen minutes day by day burned a further forty to one hundred sixty kilojoules per day. Multiply that by 365 and people kilojoules will add up!

40. Leave one thing on your plate at the top of the meal. each little counts.

Read more: The four mistakes that are creating you fat

41. once bent on eat, split a meal. The parts are typically sufficiently big to feed a family.

42. Skip course. Come on, you recognize you wish to and likelihood is you aren't even hungry after you reach for that sweet treat.

43. Don't socialise round the food tables at parties. You're a lot of doubtless to munch senselessly, even supposing you'll not be hungry.

44. Don't eat your kid's leftovers. each little of food adds up, {including|as we tend toll as|together with} what we decision "BLTs" (bites, licks and tastes).

45. Keep chips, dips and alternative high fat junk foods out of the house. It's not concerning willpower; it's about being realistic.

46. If you've got a dog, take him for a walk. It's higher for each him and you than simply holding him out the rear.

Morning within the town. Young man walking together with his do

47. If you don't have a pet, provide to run a neighbour's dog. build friends; change state.

48. Use smaller plates and bowls. there'll be less space for you to extra service and it makes less food feels like a lot of.

49. Skip buffets. It's a gone conclusion: If you don't, you'll desire you've got to urge your money's price and overindulge.

50. Slow down. It takes roughly fifteen to twenty minutes for your abdomen to sense it's full. If you wolf your food sort of a starving dog, you'll doubtless out-eat your hunger.

51. Decrease your food intake by four hundred kilojoules per day. on paper this interprets to losing nearly 450g per month (450g = fourteen 600 kilojoules) – with hardly any effort.

52. obtain a measuring instrument and accumulate a minimum of ten 000 steps day by day. It feels like everyone is doing it therefore why shouldn't you too?

53. once attainable, walk or bike to try to your errands. The additional bonus? You'll save on gasoline too.

54. Don't render bulk. The a lot of that's there, the a lot of that you'll eat.

55. Plan ahead. If you fail to arrange, you propose to fail.

56. Keep thereforeme healthy snacks – like loco – in your compartment so you're ready the least bit times.

57. Take before footage. Studies have shown that those that take weight-loss progress pics lose a lot of weight than those who don't.

58. Get new friends. If your friends like dish, wings, nachos and brewage on an everyday basis, realize friends WHO are similar and need to be healthy. analysis has recommended that friends enhance (or will hurt) success.

59. place yourself initial. many folks (women in particular) place everybody else prior themselves and let their health fall by the facet.

60. Remember: It's not all or nothing. If you fall off the bandwagon, jump right back on. Don't let yourself still fall till all progress has been lost.

61. get up early to exercise. You're a lot of doubtless to urge it done if you don't wait till once work.

If weight loss may be a goal for you, then you almost certainly already know—whether or not you would like to admit it—that there's no quickie once it involves creating it happen and making it last. perhaps you've even learned that lesson the exhausting means. (Maybe quite once.) therefore ditch the furor diets and take a glance at the massive image. It's vital to recollect that losing weight isn't concerning starving yourself, which forceful measures will place a dangerous strain on your body.

The real key to finding and maintaining a healthy weight is finding and maintaining a healthy life style. Here's some healthy-living knowledge to assist guide you on your means.

Focus on food initial.

Your initial thought may well be that you simply need to hit the athletic facility to change state, however it's not enough to figure out exhausting if you're not consumption well. analysis has found that exercise alone isn't as effective for weight loss as dietary changes. after you place them along you've got a direction for long-run success.

Eat quality calories, not empty ones.

Sugar may be a drug. however you'll kick the habit. prolong a sweets hiatus—a month is right, however do what you can —and you'll see the cravings begin to diminish. Then it'll be easier to avoid sugar-laden foods that don't offer your body the nutrients it wants, leave you hungry, and cause you to placed on weight. From there you'll focus your attention on whole grains, fruits and vegetables, fish and lean supermolecule. examine these twenty superfoods that are nice for weight loss.

And eat enough calories to really sustain you.

Your body wants food, so eat it. the thought here is to make consumption habits that you simply will really stick to, not starve yourself. If you would like to use an advert diet to assist you select what you set on your plate.

Definitely don't skip breakfast.
Eating breakfast facilitates maintain stable blood glucose levels and may help keep you full all day therefore you don't snack. In fact, a study of individuals WHO with success shed weight and unbroken it off, found that just about eighty p.c Ate breakfast a day as a part of their weight-loss strategy. Leave the croissants and muffins within the pastry shop— they really cause you to hungrier later—and elect supermolecule and whole grains to begin the day. Here are ten scrumptious protein-packed breakfasts to do. What the euphemism, here are five a lot of.

Pay attention to what you eat—literally.
They say you must watch what you eat. however what we're expression is you must really watch what you eat, as you're consumption it. inspect the food, soak up the smell and therefore the texture, relish it as you chew. It's not almost about tasting, it's concerning being aware about what you're golf shot into your body. after you dine in front of the TV or

your pc, otherwise you graze all day long at the workplace, you finish up with what primarily amounts to meal memory loss.

You don't bear in mind what you ate—and you're doubtless to eat {more|additional|a heap of} (a lot more) than you meant to. strive keeping a food diary for per week or 2 to urge to bear with what you're really consumption a day and to spot patterns that may be busybodied together with your arrange. for example, if you're continually starving by suppertime and going back for seconds and thirds, perhaps you wish to schedule in a very healthy snack at four P.M. analysis finds time and once more that observation what you eat helps you change state.

Drink tons of water and not a lot of soda, juice or alcohol. Your cells would like water to perform, therefore it's crucial to stay hydrating throughout the day. (Here are twelve straightforward ways that to drink a lot of water a day.) Yes, you'll get a number of that fluid from drinks that aren't simply plain water, however watch out that you're not gulping down loads of supernumerary calories. Soda and juice—despite its victuals content—are jam-choked with sugar. Alcohol is another supply of sneaky empty calories. If you're progressing to imbibe, strive these ten lower-calorie cocktails.

Don't skimp on sleep.

Sleep may be a astonishingly vital think about losing weight and keeping it off. those that are sleep underprivileged eat a lot of calories throughout the day and are more doubtless to place on weight.

Find a variety of exercise that you simply really need to try to.

Combining exercise with diet has been shown to be more practical for weight loss than diet alone. You'll be a lot of doubtless to stay to an everyday program of physical activity if you truly, you know, enjoy it. would like some further motivation? Get a exertion brother. You'll be less inclined to skip a run if you recognize your friend is awaiting you within the park. Here's the thin on the most effective thanks to calculate for weight loss.

And then keep doing it.

Keeping weight off may be a constant balance, and regular physical activity may be a huge a part of creating it last. You can't simply go extremely exhausting in the future and suppose, OK I'm sensible for a number of weeks. consumption healthy and exertion need to become a part of life. and that they will! and, physical activity is concerning quite simply burning off calories. you wish to strengthen your muscles, too. The cool factor is, muscles assign calories simply by existing, therefore it's solely progressing to assist you within the long haul to strengthen.

Pick up any diet book and it'll claim to carry all the answers to with success losing all the burden you want—and keeping it off. Some claim the secret's to eat less and exercise additional, others that low fat is that the solely thanks to go, whereas others order extirpation carbs. So, what must you believe?

The truth is there's no "one size fits all" answer to permanent healthy weight loss. What works for one person might not work for you, since our bodies respond otherwise to completely different foods, counting on genetic science and different health factors. to search out the strategy of weight loss that's right for you'll possible take time and need patience, commitment, and a few experimentation with completely different foods and diets.

While some folks respond well to reckoning calories or similar restrictive ways, others respond higher to having additional freedom in designing their weight-loss programs. Being absolve to merely avoid cooked foods or decrease on refined carbs will set them up for achievement.

So, don't get too discouraged if a diet that worked for someone else doesn't work for you. And don't beat yourself up if a diet proves too restrictive for you to stay with. Ultimately, a diet is merely right for you if it's one you'll be able to continue over time.

Remember: whereas there's no simple fix to losing weight, there are lots of steps you'll be able to go for develop a healthier relationship with food, curb emotional triggers to gula, and succeed a healthy weight.

Four widespread weight loss ways

1. Cut calories

Some specialists believe that with success managing your weight comes all the way down to a straightforward equation: If you eat fewer calories than you burn, you melt off. Sounds simple, right? Then why is losing weight therefore hard?

Weight loss isn't a linear event over time. once you cut calories, you will drop weight for the primary few weeks, for instance, so one thing changes. You eat identical variety of calories however you lose less weight or no weight in the least. That's as a result of once you melt off you're losing water and lean tissue moreover as fat, your metabolism slows, and your body changes in different ways in which. So, so as to continue dropping weight every week, you wish to continue cutting calories.

A calorie isn't perpetually a calorie. ingestion one hundred calories of high laevulose syrup, for instance, will have a special impact on your body than ingestion one hundred calories of broccoli. The trick for sustained weight loss is to ditch the foods that are jam-choked with calories however don't cause you to feel full (like candy) and replace them with foods that fill you up while not being loaded with calories (like vegetables).

Many people don't perpetually eat merely to satisfy hunger. we have a tendency to conjointly communicate food for comfort or to alleviate stress—which will quickly derail any weight loss arrange.

2. Cut carbs

A different means of viewing weight loss identifies the matter as not one among overwhelming too several calories, however rather the means the body accumulates fat when overwhelming carbohydrates—in explicit the role of the secretion hormone. once you eat a meal, carbohydrates from the food enter your blood as aldohexose. so as to stay your glucose levels under control, your body perpetually burns off this aldohexose before it burns off fat from a meal.

If you eat a carbohydrate-rich meal (lots of food, rice, bread, or fries, for instance), your body releases hormone to assist with the inflow of all this aldohexose into your blood. moreover as control glucose levels, hormone will 2 things: It prevents your fat cells from emotional fat for the body to burn as fuel (because its priority is to burn off the glucose) and it creates additional fat cells for storing everything that your body can't burn off. The result's that you just gain weight and your body currently needs additional fuel to burn, therefore you eat additional. Since hormone solely burns carbohydrates, you crave carbs so begins a positive feedback of overwhelming carbs and gaining weight. To melt off, the reasoning goes, you wish to interrupt this cycle by reducing carbs.

Most low-carb diets advocate commutation carbs with supermolecule and fat, that may have some negative semipermanent effects on your health. If you are doing attempt a low-carb diet, you'll be able to cut back your risks and limit your intake of saturated and trans fats by selecting lean meats, fish and eater sources of protein, low-fat farm merchandise, and ingestion lots of unifoliate inexperienced and non-starchy vegetables.

3. Cut fat

It's a mainstay of the many diets: if you don't wish to induce fat, don't eat fat. Walk down any food market aisle and you'll be bombarded with reduced-fat snacks, dairy, and packaged meals. however whereas our low-fat choices have exploded, therefore have blubber rates. So, why haven't low-fat diets worked for additional of us?

Not all fat is unhealthy. Healthy or "good" fats will really facilitate to regulate your weight, moreover as manage your moods and fight fatigue. Unsaturated fats found in avocados, nuts, seeds, soy milk, tofu, and fatty fish will facilitate fill you up, whereas adding a bit tasty oil to a plate of vegetables, for instance, will build it easier to eat healthy food and improve the general quality of your diet.

We often build the incorrect trade-offs. several people build the error of swapping fat for the empty calories of sugar and refined carbohydrates. rather than ingestion whole-fat dairy product, for example, we have a tendency to eat low- or no-fat versions that are jam-choked with sugar to create up for the loss of style. Or we have a tendency to swap our fatty breakfast bacon for a gem or doughnut that causes fast spikes in glucose.

4. Follow the Mediterranean diet

The Mediterranean diet emphasizes ingestion sensible fats and good carbs along side massive quantities of contemporary fruits and vegetables, nuts, fish, and olive oil —and solely modest amounts of meat and cheese. The Mediterranean diet is over with reference to food, though. Regular physical activity and sharing meals with others are major elements.

Whatever weight loss strategy you are attempting, it's vital to remain actuated and avoid common fasting pitfalls, like emotional ingestion.

Control emotional ingestion

We don't perpetually eat merely to satisfy hunger. only too usually, we have a tendency to communicate food once we're stressed or anxious, which may wreck any diet and put on the pounds. does one eat once you're troubled, bored, or lonely? does one snack ahead of the TV at the tip of a disagreeable day? Recognizing your emotional ingestion triggers will build all the distinction in your weight-loss efforts. If you eat once you're:

Stressed – notice healthier ways in which to calm yourself. Try yoga, meditation, or soaking during a hot bathtub.

Low on energy – notice different mid-afternoon pick-me-ups. attempt walking round the block, paying attention to energizing music, or taking a brief nap.

Lonely or bored – reach resolute others rather than reaching for the icebox. decision a follower who causes you to laugh, take your dog for a walk, or visit the library, mall, or park—anywhere there's folks.

Practice aware ingestion instead

Avoid distractions whereas ingestion. attempt to not eat whereas operating, observance TV, or driving. It's too simple to senselessly scarf out.

Pay attention. Eat slowly, feeding the smells and textures of your food. If your mind wanders, gently come your attention to your food and the way it tastes.

Mix things up to specialise in the expertise of ingestion. attempt using chopsticks instead of a fork, or use your utensils together with your non-dominant hand.

Stop ingestion before you're full. It takes time for the signal to succeed in your brain that you've had enough. Don't feel indebted to perpetually clean your plate.

Stay actuated

Permanent weight loss needs creating healthy changes to your way and food selections. to remain motivated:

Find a cheering section. Social support means that tons. Programs like Jenny Craig and Weight Watchers use cluster support to impact weight loss and long healthy ingestion. hunt down support—whether within the variety of family, friends, or a support group—to get the encouragement you wish.

Slow and steady wins the race. Losing weight too quick will take a toll on your mind and body, creating you are feeling sluggish, drained, and sick. Aim to lose one to 2 pounds every week therefore you're losing fat instead of water and muscle.

Set goals to stay you actuated. short-run goals, like desperate to work into a swimsuit for the summer, typically don't work moreover as desperate to feel more assured or become healthier for your children's sakes. once temptation strikes, specialise in the advantages you'll reap from being healthier.

Use tools to trace your progress. Smartphone apps, fitness trackers, or just keeping a journal will assist you keep track of the food you eat, the calories you burn, and also the weight you lose. Seeing the ends up in black and white will assist you keep actuated.

Get lots of sleep. Lack of sleep stimulates your craving therefore you would like additional food than normal; at identical time, it stops you feeling happy, creating you would like to stay ingestion. Sleep deprivation can even have an effect on your motivation, therefore aim for eight hours of quality sleep an evening.

Cut down on sugar and refined carbs

Whether or not you're specifically planning to cut carbs, most people consume unhealthy amounts of sugar and refined carbohydrates like bread, dish dough, pasta, pastries, white flour, white rice, and sweet breakfast cereals. commutation refined carbs with their whole-grain counterparts and eliminating candy and desserts is merely a part of the answer, though. Sugar is hidden in foods as various as canned soups and vegetables, spaghetti sauce, margarine, and plenty of reduced fat foods. Since your body gets all it wants from sugar present in food, all this superimposed sugar amounts to nada however tons of empty calories and unhealthy spikes in your blood sugar.

Less sugar will mean a slimmer waist

Calories obtained from laevulose (found in candied beverages like soda and processed foods like doughnuts, muffins, and candy) are additional possible to feature to fat around your belly. cutting short on candied foods will mean a slimmer waist moreover as a lower risk of polygenic disease.

Fill up with fruit, veggies, and fiber

Even if you're cutting calories, that doesn't essentially mean you've got to eat less food. High-fiber foods like fruit, vegetables, beans, and whole grains are higher in volume and take longer to digest, creating them filling—and nice for weight-loss.

It's usually okay to eat the maximum amount contemporary fruit and non-starchy vegetables as you want—you'll feel full before you've overdone it on the calories.

Eat vegetables raw or steamed, not cooked or breaded, and dress them with herbs and spices or a bit oil for flavor.

Add fruit to low sugar cereal—blueberries, strawberries, sliced bananas. You'll still get pleasure from voluminous sweetness, however with fewer calories, less sugar, and additional fiber.

Bulk out sandwiches by adding healthy produce selections like lettuce, tomatoes, sprouts, cucumbers, and avocado.

Snack on carrots or celery with hommmos rather than a high -calorie chips and dip.

Add additional veggies to your favorite main courses to create your dish more substantial. Even food and stir-fries will be diet-friendly if you utilize less noodles and additional vegetables.

Start your meal with dish or {vegetable thereforeup|petite marmite|minestrone|soup} to assist fill you up so you eat less of your entrée.

CHAPTER 10:

Take charge of your food setting

Set yourself up for weight-loss success by taking charge of your food environment: once you eat, what proportion you eat, and what foods you create simply on the market.

Cook your own meals reception. this permits you to regulate each portion size and what goes in to the food. building and packaged foods usually contain tons additional sugar, unhealthy fat, and calories than food parched at home—plus the portion sizes tend to be larger.

Serve yourself smaller parts. Use little plates, bowls, and cups to create your parts seem larger. Don't eat of huge bowls or directly from food containers, that makes it tough to assess what proportion you've ingested.

Eat early. Studies counsel that overwhelming additional of your daily calories at breakfast and fewer at dinner will assist you drop more pounds. ingestion a bigger, healthy breakfast will jump begin your metabolism, stop you feeling hungry throughout the day, and provides you longer to burn off the calories.

Fast for fourteen hours every day. attempt to eat dinner earlier within the day so quick till breakfast following morning. ingestion only if you're most active and giving your digestion an extended break could aid weight loss.

Plan your meals and snacks prior time. you'll be able to produce your own little portion snacks in plastic luggage or containers. ingestion on a schedule can assist you avoid eating once you aren't really hungry.

Drink additional water. Thirst will usually be confused with hunger, therefore by potable you'll be able to avoid additional calories.

Limit the quantity of tempting foods you've got reception. If you share a room with non-dieters, store indulgent foods out of sight.

Get moving

The degree to that exercise aids weight loss is receptive discussion, however the advantages go means on the far side burning calories. Exercise can increase your metabolism and improve your outlook—and it's one thing you'll be able to like right away. opt for a walk, stretch, move around and you'll have additional energy and motivation to tackle the opposite steps in your weight-loss program.

Lack time for an extended elbow grease? 3 10-minute spurts of exercise per day will be even as sensible jointly 30-minute workout.

Remember: something is best than nothing. take off slowly with little amounts of physical activity day after day. Then, as you begin to melt off and have additional energy, you'll notice it easier to become additional physically active.

Find exercise you get pleasure from. attempt walking with a follower, dancing, hiking, cycling, taking part in Frisbee with a dog, enjoying a pickup game of basketball, or taking part in activity-based video games together with your children.

Keeping the burden Off

You may have detected the wide quoted data point that 95% of individuals who melt off on a diet can regain it inside a couple of years—or even months. whereas there isn't abundant exhausting proof to support that claim, it's true that a lot of weight-loss plans fail within the future. usually that's just because diets that are too restrictive are terribly exhausting to keep up over time. However, that doesn't mean your weight loss makes an attempt are doomed to failure. aloof from it.

Since it had been established in 1994, The National Weight management written account (NWCR) within the u. s., has half-tracked over ten,000 people who have lost vital amounts of weight and unbroken it off for long periods of your time. The study has found that participants who've been thriving in maintaining their weight loss share some common ways. no matter diet you utilize to melt off within the initial place, adopting these habits could assist you to stay it off:

Stay physically active. thriving dieters within the study exercise for regarding hour, usually walking.

Keep a food log. Recording what you eat a day helps to stay you responsible and actuated.

Eat breakfast a day. most ordinarily within the study, it's cereal and fruit. ingestion breakfast boosts metabolism and staves off hunger later within the day.

Eat additional fiber and fewer unhealthy fat than the standard yank diet.

Regularly check the size. deliberation yourself weekly could assist you to notice any little gains in weight, sanctionative you to promptly take corrective action before the matter escalates.

Watch less tv. cutting short on the time spent sitting ahead of a screen will be a key a part of adopting a additional active way and preventing weight gain.

Conclusion

E motional eating is when individuals use diet as a way of dealing with emotions, rather than fulfilling hunger. We've all been there, stopping out of frustration or downing cookie after cookie with a whole bag of chips while cramming for a big test. But emotional eating may affect weight, safety, and overall well-being when done a lot. But now you have all the information needed inside this books to overcome all the difficulties along you journey to be free!

CPSIA information can be obtained
at www.ICGtesting.com
Printed in the USA
BVHW041027280121
598992BV00005B/38